Praise for

Twice Born

"Hester Kaplan does with memoir what her acclaimed father, Justin, did with biography—finds the right subject, makes it new, and teaches us how to write with great compassion and grace." —Annie Dillard, Pulitzer Prize–winning author of *Pilgrim at Tinker Creek*

"Justin Kaplan was a brilliant biographer and a role model for many of us. In this intimate and unflinching look at her oh-so-private father, Hester Kaplan makes clear she has inherited Justin's genes for understated, artful, and illuminating narrative." —Larry Tye, author of *Bobby Kennedy: The Making of a Liberal Icon*

"In this acutely observed, beautifully drawn portrait, Hester Kaplan searches for her eminent biographer father through his work—especially on Mark Twain—as well as through his silences, secrets, and her own vivid memories. And with deep, imaginative empathy, she finds him." —Jean Strouse, author of *Family Romance: John Singer Sargent and the Wertheimers*

"While the course of a life once lived cannot be changed, its meaning can be, and that magic happens here. A loving daughter draws on a deep well of feeling, and a skilled writer draws on hard-earned wisdom, to bring irresistibly to life the ingenious but wounded figures of her unforgotten father, of his greatest subject—and of Hester Kaplan herself, who is every bit their match. Exquisite biography. Heartrending memoir. Twice born. Twice blest."

—James Carroll, author of *An American Requiem: God, My Father, and the War That Came Between Us*

"A magnificent combination of memoir and biography, *Twice Born* is a work of reconciliation and a resurrection of the extraordinary man who gave us Mark Twain, Walt Whitman, and at last, through his daughter's magic, his own passionate heart." —Megan Marshall, Pulitzer Prize–winning author of *Margaret Fuller: A New American Life*

Twice Born

Twice Born

Finding My Father
in the Margins of Biography

•

HESTER KAPLAN

Catapult
New York

TWICE BORN

First Catapult edition: 2025

The estate of Justin Kaplan grants permission to
use excerpts from the following works:
Mr. Clemens and Mark Twain by Justin Kaplan;
Mark Twain and His World by Justin Kaplan;
Back Then by Anne Bernays and Justin Kaplan;
The Book of Names by Anne Bernays and Justin Kaplan

ISBN: 978-1-64622-309-1

Library of Congress Control Number: 2025937425

Jacket design and illustration by Victoria Maxfield
Book design by Wah-Ming Chang

Catapult
New York, NY
books.catapult.co

Printed in the United States of America

1 3 5 7 9 10 8 6 4 2

To my sisters

A Note About Quotes

Each chapter of this memoir opens with a quote from Justin Kaplan's writing on Mark Twain: his Pulitzer Prize— and National Book Award—winning biography, *Mr. Clemens and Mark Twain*, published in 1966 by Simon & Schuster; and his second book on the author, *Mark Twain and His World*, published in 1974 by Simon & Schuster.

Twice Born

One

Navigating

●

"To the end he remained as much an enigma and prodigy to himself as he was to the thousands at the Brick Presbyterian Church in New York who filed past the casket, topped with a single wreath of laurel, where he lay in a white suit."

From the moment I was aware of my father's existence as separate from my own, I have been trying to find him. He was always present in my life but always hidden from me, and on the morning of his cremation in 2014, given the circumstances of corpse and casket in front of me, I no more expected some profound discovery than I expected him to sit up in his cardboard box and tell me one of his dirty jokes. What I did know was that for a few minutes I would be free to gaze at him without either of us looking away the moment our lack of connection and inability to speak to and about each other and ourselves came into full relief. The crematorium director was clearly tickled that this morning's body was Justin Kaplan, the acclaimed biographer of Mark Twain and Walt Whitman, among others. He had read all of my father's books, he said, as he lifted the lid off the casket and backed out of the room so that my father and I could "spend some time alone."

My husband, Michael, was with me, but neither my older sister, Susanna, nor my younger sister, Polly, nor my mother, Anne, had considered coming. I didn't question their choice, but they robustly questioned mine, which seemed gruesome and unfathomable to them. My answer was simple: I wanted to see the body off and I wanted to know myself as it happened. There are times when the certainty of the only chance has its own propulsive force. Bravery has nothing to do with it. My father had been sick with Parkinson's for years and plagued by frequent bouts of pneumonia; at eighty-eight, his death was not tragic or unexpected.

I didn't know what to call this chilly, high-ceilinged space we were in besides *antechamber*, though the only place this one led was to one of the three ovens on the far wall. The casket was pointed headfirst in that direction so there'd be no question about what your business was here. Like a plane on the tarmac waiting for takeoff, I might have said to my father, like a dog at the door waiting to be let out, snout against the glass, he might have countered. Had he been breathing, we might have talked about what a better name was for where he now waited, eternally patient as he wasn't when he was alive, in a faded hospital gown, identical to the one I'd last seen him in. We would have agreed that the words *oven* and *chamber* were problematic, particularly together, and he might have given his Jewish shrug, half enduring pride, half enduring pain. And then we'd have tossed out some ideas: the Proofing Room or the Preboarding Area. And there would be nothing ghoulish about this and no offense meant, though my father might take some pleasure in making a person squirm a bit if any sensitive onlooker had been around.

Death was death and we didn't invent it. Always tell the truth about it, my father insisted. People didn't pass away. They didn't kick the bucket or buy the farm or go to a better place: they died. They were dead. Use language precisely. He had been an orphan by thirteen. His mother had died when he was six, his father seven years later, both of them from cancer, and he'd been raised by his older brother Howard, his aunt Frances, and Georgia Edwards, who had worked as the family's longtime housekeeper. My father knew the ache that huddled in euphemism, even if he wouldn't ever talk about his parents, his experience of loss, and what he'd done with all that weight that had fallen on him. Even if that was what I had always wanted to know from and about him— nothing short of how you live when you know too early how it ends, and could end too soon—even if it was the source and shape of his creative drive, and I suspect today in my search for him, the source of my own.

Twain had said that the New England weather was "always doing something there; always attending strictly to business; always getting up new designs and trying them on the people to see how they will go." There had been a storm the night before, an April event designed to tease, and through the room's high, clean windows, I watched branches heavy with snow spring up as the sun released them from their loads. I thought that when we were done, Michael and I might walk through Mount Auburn Cemetery on the sparkling wet blacktop and find the graves of Fannie Farmer of cookbook fame, Red Sox announcer Curt Gowdy, John Bartlett of the quotations (one of my father's heroes), B. F. Skinner of the box, Mary Baker Eddy (whose double-noun name confused me), and Henry Wadsworth Longfellow, to name just a few of the heavy hitters. To be dead on the same grounds of the buried esteemed in Cambridge, Massachusetts, a city where accomplishment, expertise, and intellect were sacred above all else, in this cemetery where we'd often gone as a family of five and tossed a pink rubber ball over the humorless headstones, would have pleased my father but made him uneasy too, evidence of his desire for recognition and his distrust of approbation, his feelings of being an outsider still after all these ascendant decades as a writer and literary figure in a literary city, and his squeamishness at belonging to anything.

A bird hovered at the glass as if to remind me to get to it already: *Look at him. It's what you came to do.* I was stalling then and I'm stalling now. If you want to write, observe everything, my mother, a novelist and nonfiction writer, had instructed me as a child. No one cares about the sunny days, she had also said, a piece of advice I wonder if I've taken too much to heart in my writing, because it is the struggle against those dark clouds that has always interested me and appeared in my stories. But observation—of the immaculate tile floor and the puddle of melted snow around my boots, the shine of the oven doors that resisted reflection, the burning under my ribs, the smell of pine—is also a great means of avoidance, and one that felt particularly familiar when it came to how my father and I interacted.

All my life, on those instances when we were alone together, we observed what was in front of us: a woman's funny shoes, drivers struggling to parallel park, the way fat grows opaque on a pot of cooling soup. In the summer, we sometimes stood side by side on the deck looking out over Cape Cod Bay and talked about the shifting hues of water, how writers and painters had attempted to depict these things, and once about how the narrator of *A High Wind in Jamaica*, one of his favorite childhood books, had said, "Writers have often lost their way trying to explain how brilliant a jewel the humming-bird is: it cannot be done."

But we didn't talk about our own attempts at capturing the hummingbird in words, an aspiration that we shared even before I began to write, and we never faced each other or found comfortable or honest footing together because we were too alike: shy, cripplingly private, overly vulnerable, hoarders of our true selves. And because it seemed he had always sensed my deep longing to unwrap the secret of him, he was then—and was still now, a half century later in his casket—unable and unwilling to look directly at me.

It's not easy to force the eyes to take in the dead body, but there it was, finally. Having done it didn't release me from feeling the pull to turn away, and my gaze was almost impossible to hold. I found some compromise in a crouch low enough to see how my father's nose arced toward the horizon line of the casket's edge. An interviewer had written that it was a "prominent proboscis," which my father had laughed at for its clumsy attempt at sounding sophisticated, though I suspected it also hurt him some. Tell the truth about that, too; he had an extraordinarily weird nose, shaped like no other in the history of noses. If you'd seen it once, you wouldn't have forgotten it. Run down it from the forehead and it looked classically humped and semitically descendant, but move toward the elongated nostrils and come to a sudden, screeching stop. The tip of his nose was entirely flat, a circle slightly smaller than a dime, as though when the flesh was still malleable he'd walked into a wall. It was a nose that drew stares, smirks, and questions, and I could never look at it without experiencing a tinge of embarrassment for both of us. My mother had said that women found it sexy. Pictures of him as a boy reveal a more normally tapered nose; he claimed this prominence of cartilage had only begun to appear when he was in his midtwenties. Despite this, I'd always believed that his orphanhood was somehow responsible for his honker, as he called it, that some normal growth process had been sharply distorted by the early death of his parents. Half-formed, abruptly halted. He had slammed into the border that separated his before and after.

His strong chin was roughed with stubble and his thin mouth gave the impression of erudition, equanimity, playfulness, and gentle amusement, which is what he presented to the world. He was modest and charming and people were always drawn to him. If asked, he might share his opinion of a bloviating politician (his favorite kind, ripe for ridicule) or a pretentious movie (his least favorite kind), or he might offer you a literary nugget pulled from the vast library in his head to make his point. You might note his silk pocket square, get a whiff of his 4711 cologne, and conclude that he seemed comfortable in his place in the world, but that it was impossible to ever know what he was feeling. He kept that to himself. His hair, not yet fully gray, was a patch of closely buzzed fuzz, and in the lacy light of the antechamber, his skin looked smooth and robust, his cheeks animated by dimples. The severe eczema that had plagued him his entire life—he told me he thought he'd scratched even in utero—had spared his face, but evidence of the condition peeked out at the gown's mint-green neckline. His hands had always been busy scratching himself, even in his sleep, and his arms and legs often displayed constellations of scabs where he'd gone too hard at skin thinned and purpled by steroid creams.

Looking at my father's body, I thought of the "The Invalid's Story," one of Twain's short pieces he had handed me as a kid; he was always giving me things to read, often without explanation. A train's expressman, in the presence of a coffin making its final journey home, says of the corpse, "Sometimes it's uncertain whether they're really gone or not—seem gone, you know—body warm, joints limber—and so, although you think they're gone, you don't really know. I've had cases in my car. It's perfectly awful, becuz you don't know what minute they'll rise up and look at you!"

I'd always loved the grisly and funny tale (the narrator mistakes the smell of Limburger cheese for a decomposing body), and even as a child, I had found solace in the possibility that the dead aren't really dead. But there was no such wishful uncertainty this morning as the years collapsed around me, child and adult at the same time as I stood over my father.

Maybe, too, it was my father's finally settled hands—no need to soothe the tormenting itch or scribble down notes with his treasured gold pencil—that attuned me to a different kind of sureness that morning. We aren't aware of the minute vibrations in the body, the lip's pulse, the flutter of the eyelid, the rise of gooseflesh, all the seemingly imperceptible sensations of the living, but we are acutely aware of the absence of them in the dead as we become as alert as animals to the stillness of blood. What we notice too is that the dead don't sense us near them. They don't register our own vibrations thrown into an electric arrhythmia, and all our scrutiny of them, our curiosity, confusion, disappointment, gratitude, love, all those elements that charge and enrich the air between the living, are thrown back at us with alarming velocity. It was all mine alone now, unresolved and ravenous. I wondered what to do with all this uncaged, crackling energy, if it might compel me to continue the search to know my father's life after it was over, to feel what it felt to be him. But to what end? Should I instead just let this desire burn up and float away?

We? I? Did you notice how you're switching points of view here? my (dead) father might have asked if he were reading this, but he wouldn't ask me why I was doing it.

So please ask me *why*, Joe (which is what my sisters and I only ever called him), and I will tell you, as I sit here at my desk, that it's because switching points of view can be like stepping into a familiar room through an unfamiliar doorway, and I've stepped out of myself at this moment of writing to invite you to join me in this venture to find you. After all, this is exactly what you did with the subjects of your biographies.

It's not the first look at the corpse that shocks so much; it is the one after that when the impact doubles down and gives you a last chance at a different take before the casket is closed. "The bodies of the newly dead are not debris nor remnant, nor are they entirely icon or essence," Thomas Lynch, a deeply sympathetic writer suggests. "They are, rather, changelings, incubates, hatchlings of a new reality." As I looked over the new reality of my father, the atmosphere grew warm with the breath of his long-gone parents. Death, I understood then, had always been present, standing between us in the form of their absence, and I missed people I had never met, people he never talked about and whose names he never spoke. Now Tobias and Anna, stoic, pious, and thick-shouldered, wept openly over their youngest boy lying there in that terrible hospital gown, in that cheap cardboard casket, the man they never saw grow up.

Come back to us, they said.

I couldn't look anymore, and Michael went to collect the director who was standing out in the hall, the man's job as much about patience as anything else. When he came back in to close the casket, I asked him how long most people stayed with the body. Everyone is different, he said, diplomatically. I peppered him with other questions, which was the best trick I'd learned from my father to avoid scrutiny of myself and the uncomfortable moment. What happens next? How long does a cremation take? How is the fire lit? Then what? What I really wanted to understand was, had I spent enough time, and enough time for what exactly? Growing up, I'd had no experience in the protocols and discussions of death. My parents avoided hospital and sickbed visits, widows and widowers, funerals and condolence calls, and even telling me when my mother's mother had died when I was in college. I'd had to discover the news in the morning paper while I waited at a counter for my coffee.

"Are you a writer too?" the director asked.

I wiggled away from his question. Having grown up with two parents who were writers at the center of a writing universe, and who deemed themselves judges on who did and who didn't get to call themselves one, I have never called myself a writer. Even today the designation makes me uneasy, and at most I say I am someone who writes, though I have published books, stories, and essays, won awards and fellowships and invitations. It is what I spend my time doing and teaching and thinking about.

The director said that the day before, knowing who he'd be attending to this morning, he had read more about my father, and he detailed for me his many awards and accomplishments, among them the National Book Award and Pulitzer Prize for his Twain biography, the first book he'd ever written. It was an astonishing achievement, we both agreed. Given the man's willingness to discuss the mechanics of cremation with me, I suspected he believed that writers, like crematory directors, were by professional necessity able to keep at bay the avalanche of sentiment that threatens to bury us at any moment.

Threaten to bury us? my father might have whispered to me. *Who exactly is us?*

I'm just holding back the avalanche, I might have whispered in return. *Get used to it. Feel its power pushing back? That's where writing's tools are forged.*

The director called in his assistant and they closed the casket and slid it through the now open oven door. The process had all the choreographed efficiency of the pizza place on Huron Avenue on a busy weeknight where you might see some of Cambridge's most illustrious residents ordering double cheese and pepperoni. Taking us to the room behind the ovens, the director asked if I'd like to push the button that turned on the flames. Once again, certainty exerted its force, and I knew this was the one and only time I'd ever be able to do this. And really, who would want to do it more than that? The button was resistant, as if giving me a chance to change my mind, and it required a more resolute jab. There was a click, then a vacuum of silence, and then a whoosh as the flames took shape. Through a small metal hatch that the director swung aside as if we were at a peep show, I watched the flames erect blue and orange fencing around the casket. That was enough. I let the hatch swing back in place.

I saw the room where the ashes—not my father's, not this soon—were delivered. "My father had a hip replacement," I said to the director. "Titanium. What happens to that?"

Some families want to keep the pieces that aren't devoured by flame (Joe would have appreciated how perfect that word *devoured* was at that moment, delighting in the industry's lugubrious lexicon), but some don't, he explained, and those bits are sold to recyclers, the money given to charity. Suppose, I might have said to Joe, the charity was one the dead person detested, like the ASPCA for the woman who poisoned the neighborhood dogs with antifreeze, or UNICEF for the man who screamed at kids. We would have made a game of it, written a list and hung it on the refrigerator, invited others to contribute, ranked the entries and jockeyed for top billing. In our attempt to outsmart and disarm, we would have skillfully ignored the fact that we were talking about what death leaves behind when all else is gone—bits of metal and a lot of mystery. I told the director that I would like to keep my father's titanium joint. Had he been alive, Joe might have used it as a paperweight, but he had no papers to hold down anymore. Or rather, there were papers still on his desk, just where he'd left them as though he believed he'd be back in a few minutes, but why bother to constrain or order them now? Or he might have put the joint on the kitchen table to provoke a reaction, with any luck an uncomfortable one, from his many friends who sat there. I might use the thing still to keep my study door from slamming shut or as a weight to compress the mud of my thoughts into shale. (I have fully entered the still-speculative language I use to talk about aborted plans and the freshly dead; *I might have, had he not been dead, he might have.*)

I was desperate to get out into the air. Had he been alive, my father might have noticed that when we left the crematory, the sky was a piercing blue. (My father's blue eyes had been closed; no surprise, he had not opened them and gazed back at me from his casket.) He might have looked up and been as relieved as I was not to see the smoke of himself spiraling into the squint-inducing brightness of the day. That didn't mean he wasn't there, though, drifting down Mount Auburn Street, passing Star Market where he liked to shop, the liquor store where he bought his off-brand vodka, on his way to the apartment building where he'd lived with my mother for the past few years, and where on the ninth floor she waited for me to return, though she'd never ask for details of the morning. Then, lifted on a breeze from the Charles River, Joe drifted through Harvard Square and Harvard Yard, down Kirkland Street to Francis Avenue, and up the front steps of the house where he'd lived for over half a century and raised his three daughters and done his work day after grinding day, through the front entrance and the double doors to his study and to the bookshelf facing the desk, the pencil, the paper, finally settling between the covers of the books he'd written.

In the year after Joe died, I wrote a story called "The Biographer." The unambiguous title was there before I'd even written a word, suggesting that I might be stepping into a new arena. The male characters I'd written before always had facets of him, hints, habits, and a familiar opacity, his life's details about beloved dogs choking on pork chop bones, lilacs, red kayaks in Cape Cod Bay, lost nephews. I wrote about men who were susceptible to bouts of melancholy, husbands and fathers who wondered as they got older if they'd missed their opportunity to understand the people who loved them, men who hid from the repercussions of their own emotions. But with "The Biographer," I thought I might come face-to-face with him and finally resist his need to hide and resist my own to allow it.

In the story, an aging biographer is agitated and at loose ends because his computer has locked him out of his work, even as he suspects he has no more real work left to do. His wife of five decades chirps familiarly behind him. Over the course of the stymieing day, he stands on a ninth-floor balcony above the Charles River and contemplates why he's spent his entire career as a biographer trying to know the lives of his subjects when he has so determinedly avoided trying to know his own. He doesn't know why he never looked back to discover how he'd weathered the deaths of his parents as a boy, how he'd spent years wandering and desperate for the let-up of grief, and how he'd navigated his way to work, love, and this exact moment. As he waits for a visit from his grandson, he understands that he has also avoided knowing his three daughters and hidden himself from them in the process. He senses the work ahead of him, though the afternoon is growing cold and the wind whips up from the water, and the bridge between his then and now, his lost and regained, might be impossible to cross this late. The most he can do is remember, reframe, and touch his grandson's cheek.

While writing the story, I hoped for the conflagrations and consolations of fiction—the satisfying freedom to make up and make sense of what doesn't yield neatly or comfortably in real life: meaning, causality, motivation, the still core of the character. When the piece was finished, I cried at the depths of pain I'd revealed, but I saw that the story was incomplete, familiar in its rhythms and territory of reluctance, a half step into honesty, but still a defter, more seasoned step out of it. My father believed that for Twain, fiction had become "a delicately controlled illusion in which the 'truth,' in order to be believed, had to be disguised as a lie." The same was true for "The Biographer." I had, in the end, lost courage and looked away first.

When I read the piece to a university audience one night, I felt that I had abandoned that cranky protagonist out on the balcony with his new clarity about all he wouldn't be able to fix. And that like him, I saw that I also hadn't explored *how* he'd gotten to that moment—how he had come to work, to love, to harness the power of his past—the essential mysteries of the biographer, the character, and I realized, the essential mysteries of the biographer, my father.

Beyond the audience shrugging on their coats when the reading was over, a window framed a biting winter night in Rhode Island and I imagined my father making his way across the lit and icy parking lot in his faded parka so he might ask me to read my story out loud to him and finally talk to me about my work. I had never shown him or asked him to read what I'd written, including my novels and story collections, because I was as afraid of being exposed by my words and imagination as I was of falling short of his impossible standards of writing, reference, and originality—standards I had internalized often to a point of paralysis. This was a man who savored Proust, Roth, *Mad* magazine, dictionaries, psychology, philosophy, and endless amounts of poetry. The biographer in my story desired that "no one would ever write a biography of him. He preferred ignorance, self-blindness, the suspense of his own story," and now I was afraid of all he might recognize about himself and my breach of his privacy in the face of his determination to stay unexamined. But if I were finally brave enough, I needed to hear everything he felt about this story, what about it mattered to him, moved and reminded him, maybe even revealed some of the truths of his own life to him. I needed to know how he saw my attempts to capture him, if I'd gotten any of it right and any of it wrong. I needed to hear what it helped him understand about me.

But this imagined moment with all its earnest fictional trickery of parking lot apparitions would have made my father shake his head. *Too easy*, he might say, *too predictable, and worse than that, not true.* These are my pages, though, and I'll resist his posthumous and picky red penciling and say that who I *actually* saw out there was a shivering, restive woman in her midfifties who looked an awful lot like me. Her children were grown, her mother was old and fierce, her work was losing its pulse, her long marriage bruised. She had so many secrets and sorrows and shames that she'd never told anyone about, cloaking herself in them and in a false confidence whose heat alone should have melted the ice under her feet.

That woman understands that this is how grief's dogged search party hunts you down, sometimes in a parking lot, or on a balcony above a slow river, or in a supermarket aisle at midnight with no sense of what you're looking for or even what you're missing. But that woman also suspects that it is a great and painful fortune to be found at such a moment in her life when she can look at herself and ask, *What are you saving all that heartache and longing and honesty for? Why are you hoarding its power?* She understands this: her father is the story she's always wanted to find and tell; she's just been dancing around it for too long.

"The way to write," Emerson said, "is to throw your body at the mark when your arrows are spent." It was time for me to get to it, to throw my body at the mark and write a different kind of story of my father, a biography of a biographer, and a biography of a parent.

As I left the reading, I recalled how on the day of his cremation, my father's vaporous navigation had led me back to the house on Francis Avenue, to his study below my childhood bedroom that I still imagine when I'm failing to fall asleep, to his shelves, and to the books he'd written, the ones I'd never read when he was alive. And now I heard him say to me, *Look. This is where I've always been, this where you need to start, this is where you'll find me. Open my book and read.*

Two

Cracking the Spine

•

"He learned to 'read' the water as he read a book and to know that shape of the river so well that he could steer at night 'the way you follow a hall at home in the dark. Because you know the shape of it.'"

From its publication in 1966 when I was seven, my own copy—because I insisted on having one—of *Mr. Clemens and Mark Twain*, my father's first book, was always with me, no matter how old I was or where I lived. I knew its width, the off-white hue of its textured jacket, and its exact location, sometimes next to my collection of Trolls, scented candles, and tiny glass animals, later next to bottles of perfume, a broken Timex a boy had given me, later next to the books I'd written. But in all the years, I'd never cracked the book's spine, turned the pages, or smelled the ink. Closed, sealed, intact, the book was an object of unplumbed meaning.

My father rarely asked anyone for anything, not for comfort, a glass of water, or even to pull the shade down so the sun wouldn't hit him in the eye, and he never asked me to read his books. That he also seemed not to have any expectation that I would—it simply never came up—offered me a useful rationale for why I didn't: if my opinion didn't matter to him, then my opinion couldn't possibly matter. Let David McCullough, Annie Dillard, Kurt Vonnegut, John Updike, Bernard Malamud, and an ever-expanding pantheon of successful writers, editors, and critics—who seemed to have read every book on earth and remember every line—give him their opinions as they sat around our long kitchen table, while my father stirred a pot of chili on the stove and hid his blushing and uneasiness at their praise. I was always standing just out of sight, listening greedily to how it was you thought and talked about books and writing, and monitoring my mother's brightly envious expression.

My reasoning for not reading my father's books, familiar in its legacy of self-effacement, his and mine, also let me off the hook because there was risk attached: What if I did read them but didn't *get* them? What if I read them wrong, or if I didn't know enough of anything to make sense of what they were really about? What if I wasn't smart enough, and would never be like those friends around the table?

I can recall with the endlessly rechargeable heat that comes with humiliation my father's dismay at my reading of Browning's "My Last Duchess," a middle school assignment. He rarely helped with my homework (and I rarely asked), but I was stuck that night. I knew what I *thought* I was reading and what the poem was about, but how could I be sure? How was anyone ever sure? Under his urging to "just look at what's there, for fuck's sake," I stopped seeing anything at all and could only hear him breathing with noisy distress through his nose. Nothing provoked the kind of disappointment that being a lazy reader and thinker did—even if that reader and thinker was a child. That I was intimidated into blankness would not have occurred to him. In a house where reading was assumed and reading well was the standard to be measured by, where you could rise, fall, or be marked by ignorance, indifference, and dopiness, these fears were real possibilities, and the judgment passed was unshakable. In this world of writers, books, and book talk I already doubted I could ever enter, I kept my unvetted observations about what I read to myself, storing them away like secrets and wishes made out of nothing but gauze and girlish impressions.

But this isn't the whole explanation. People had always been surprised by my not having read my father's books as though it signaled some stinginess, lack of gratitude, or pathology on my part. *If my father had written a book*, they say. *If my parents were writers*, they say. But they don't know. They don't know that the child of the parent-writer understands that it's not only impossible to separate the work from the writer, but also, uniquely, to separate the *child* from the writer. The child recognizes the parent-writer's narrative choices, mirroring, forks, intersections, and details, and what strikes her as false or untrue, she labels as hypocrisy, distortion, or misunderstanding, not invention, imagination, or creation. What strikes her as revelation often comes with the stinging slap of a new reality. As the daughter of two successful writers, this was not conflation or confusion on my part. This was a different kind of reader's truth and was the life of the writer's child, something my father, even as a young father himself, already understood when he wrote about Twain's daughter Susy's dislike for her father's story "The Golden Arm." Not only did the story about a dead wife terrify the girl, but "there were implicit parallels that were bound to set up some disturbing subliminal vibrations . . . [for] an anxious and sensitive child."

I was an anxious and sensitive child too, self-conscious about the beige adhesive eye patch I wore for years to correct a lazy eye, then later the thick glasses that slid down my nose. Even having never read a page of my father's book, I knew the vibrations wouldn't be subliminal for me. I knew because I'd experienced this with my mother's novels, having read them from too young an age because she'd demanded I (and never my sisters) do so, my father quietly begging me to comply in order to placate her and restore peace in the house. Her books became a weapon aimed at the heart of our relationship and my autonomy: to not read her work was to not love her. I knew the vibrations because I was incapable of separating her characters' sex lives, sentiments, and judgments from her own, or ignoring the disconnect between the scene she'd written and the way I knew it had actually happened. In one novel, she wrote about a daughter who travels to Europe with her boyfriend and doesn't call home, sending the mother into a frenzy of fury, worry, and finally disparagement. I had gone to Europe with a boyfriend when I was twenty-one and she'd been angry that I hadn't called enough, but her characterization of the girl as cruel and selfish and the boy as callous and spoiled was deeply unkind, a betrayal, and a domination of her narrative over mine.

"But it's fiction," she said when I pushed back about the portrayal one morning at breakfast during a visit home, the offending chapter still fresh in my mind from having read it the night before. A successful writing career stood behind her like a henchman. In showing her *how* I'd read, what I'd been affected by and identified with, I'd made the mistake of revealing myself and my susceptibilities to her, her work, and how she viewed me, things I had always been on guard against. My father, busy removing the yarmulke shell from his hard-boiled egg and always averse to conflict, even at my expense, shrugged and kept silent.

There was an aura of reverence around the writers my parents admired (dead and alive), and they assumed their children would feel the same way. Bernard Malamud, who lived nearby in the late 1960s when he was teaching at Harvard, would often drop in. Years later, I would hear my father describe to friends how Malamud would sit next to my younger sister, Polly, on the couch and invent fantastical stories for her. After one of these visits, she'd begged my father, please, she didn't want to hear any more stories about Jewish bears in sneakers.

"Polly had no idea how lucky she was," he would add in the telling. But I was the one who'd watched her squirm during these sessions when she was made captive by my father's awe for the man and gratification in the scene.

As young girls of six and eight, my older sister, Susanna, and I received an invitation from P. L. Travers, author of *Mary Poppins*, on salmon-colored card stock with a drawing of her titular character, bag in one hand, black umbrella in the other, lifting skyward, to "Tea in the New Year for Tiny Children." My nervous father, in a jacket and tie, stood on the periphery with the other wide-eyed parents while my sister and I sat on a dusty carpet in the living room of a Radcliffe House Master with other subdued children, eating dry cookies off heavy plates. In advance, I had been told in breathless terms that I would be in the presence of a very important writer, but when the moment came, I was only concerned with the fact that P. L. Travers wasn't actually Mary Poppins/Julie Andrews.

The "luck" and value of these literary encounters, of which there were many during my childhood, was fully in the eyes of my parents, who felt they were a gift to us—*Kids, come say hello to Carlos Fuentes, Saul Bellow, Betty Friedan, Mary Oliver, Anatole Broyard, and then step back, be quiet, listen, learn, observe, absorb.* They remembered dinner with V. S. Pritchett, lunch with Peter Taylor, an evening with Lillian Hellman, another with Pauline Kael, one with Robert Frost, who recited poetry. They had met Leonard Woolf, Elizabeth Bishop, Nadine Gordimer. Updike sometimes sat in the kitchen and watched golf on the tiny black-and-white television and a few times attempted to help me with my math homework. My severe ineptitude with numbers was humiliating and I wanted to escape, but as the charmed writer's hand rested on the child's muddled head, and his other hand reached for the eraser to remedy her mistakes, the parents felt they too were lucky.

My parents talked about books endlessly—their own included—as though they were the most important things in the world. They read out loud to each other, one of the love rites of their marriage that happened within the swirl of family life and three daughters who wanted to plug their ears and turn on the television instead. Within the privacy and confines of the house, my parents saw no useful boundary between the writer and the work when they talked, so when I read their friends' books, which I always did, even when I didn't always understand what I was reading, I also knew just how these people who wrote about attraction or history or opera singers or science or cities sat on our wobbly chairs, fought with their spouses in front of others, had tumors in their breasts, slipped on our front steps and looked around to make sure no one had seen, because I witnessed all of it. I knew how these writers were kind or dismissive to me, how they petted the dog or nudged it away, how they picked up the dropped cashew or kicked it under the couch. I knew how they talked about their triumphs and humiliations in exquisite detail. *I was so drunk I beshat myself in the back seat of the limo*, an acclaimed writer announced over lunch in the kitchen one Saturday. (The word *beshat* was a miracle to me.) She'd been on her way to a ceremony where she was receiving a major award. *And I was wearing an Ultrasuede pantsuit!* she added, laughing. Was this what it meant to be a writer? I knew how these writers postured and demurred, that they had money problems, romance woes, runs in their stockings, and siblings they hated. I knew how the best-selling writer whose novel would become a television series announced with pride that his girlfriend had dumped him because she was jealous of his success. I knew how the man who let his cigarette ash fall on our living room rug had also written about the scent of a baby's fontanel so evocatively that it stirred up for me a pre-pubescent urge to have a child as well as an urge to see him with his clothes off. I knew how the writer who'd come to a party wearing a jacket covered with cat hair had written a devastatingly spare scene of instant tragedy—a toddler killed by a car on a country road while his parents had their backs turned. I buried that novel at the bottom of a pile by my bed, then took it out to read the scene over and over because of its ability to make me feel each time newly as though all the air had gone out of my body, and wonder how words could do that. The man who'd written about weapons of war talked about the female orgasm while spreading salmon mousse on a cracker. I knew how the poet let his wife tie his shoes for him, how the novelist who talked incessantly about herself had written about what you might hear at night in the woods if you were quiet enough to listen, a revelation that kept me alert to the sounds of city violence. I'd watched a short story writer slip a pack of Juicy Fruit gum into his pocket while his groceries were being bagged at Savenor's on Kirkland Street. There was mystery and magic in how the meekest of these writers in person could also be the bravest on the page, the brute could also be the angel, the modest could be giant, the ordinary and bowed could be extraordinary.

"In homes where the near friends and visitors are mainly

literary people . . . the children's ears become early familiar-ized with wide vocabularies," Twain had written. Hovering around the edges of my parents' parties, and believing I was invisible, I paid attention and learned not only the words but also the gestures of adult life. Maybe it was the coveted in-vitation itself, or the setting of the old house bursting with benign domestic mess, dogs, cats, kids, and the casualness of how our privacy was made entirely public on party days that made guests let down their guard and act out their dramas. I'd watched a man and woman make out on the narrow back stairs that ran off the kitchen while their spouses were in the other room. Another time I heard a writer ask if he could lick the scar that filigreed a woman's neck. One guest had a full-blown emotional collapse at the tail end of an evening and hid behind the living room couch until an ambulance came and took her away, her husband looking on and shaking his head. I couldn't tell if he was distressed, embarrassed, or relieved. At eight, I had crouched under the dining room table during one of my parents' parties and watched a man's hand make his way under a woman's skirt and disappear between her legs. Above me, knives scraped plates and people laughed. The next morning, I told my parents what I'd seen and they excitedly tried to reconstruct who had been sitting where. In becoming listening device, hidden camera, notebook, I had discovered that I could hold a hundred stories.

An acclaimed and popular writer often came to the many cocktail and dinner parties my parents hosted. On one of these evenings when I was about thirteen, I watched him put his hand on the small of his wife's back and guide her toward the drinks. She must have felt a tiny chill when the cold green silk of her blouse pressed against her skin, while he must have felt her warmth through it, even as I could see how tensely she held herself. I was sure of this because I had just finished reading his latest novel, already reviewed on the front page of *The New York Times Book Review*, and it had opened my eyes to the millions of telling clues you might detect in even the smallest gestures and glances if you chose to pay attention.

As the novelist poured his wife a careful glass of red wine, I recalled how his narrator had observed the lengthening of a woman's calf as she bent at the waist to pick up a child's toy from the floor. For an instant, he had also spotted the white flash of her cotton panties when her dress lifted, and he imagined the scent of her pubic hair, so unlike his wife's. It had been a thrilling and vaguely terrifying thing for me to read and swallow whole, a glimpse at how adults behaved, what they were driven by and what and who they could destroy with their writing. And what hid behind their ordinary poses, station wagons, credit card bills, antacids. But that night I also saw on the face of the novelist's wife how pride and humiliation had collided to mangle something inside her. It was a look I would never forget, one I'd see other women try to hide my whole life. When she shakily filled a glass with water at the sink, I saw that she couldn't find her own comfort anymore, and certainly not here in this house ever again, among all these readers. When she looked at me and smiled, uneasiness shook me like a fever.

Yes, my parents said, when I brought it up the next morning in the kitchen where glasses and dishes remained from the night before, *he screws around. Always has. But boy, he can write!*

I heard stories about the finest male writers (never the women) who were faithless rogues and seducers, men whose bad behavior was thought to be the fountain of their creativity. Shut off the source, and they would be left staring at the blank page. I knew these men; they sat at my parents' table and were fed, rocked back in their chairs and brayed and ogled. One had asked my father within my earshot if he was "making good use" of our long-legged, blond babysitter.

I saw that the psychological integration of writer and word, as problematic as it could be, was also necessary to writing that was worth anything. Writers used what was in front of them: the chill in bed, the emptied bank account, the burnt toast, the abortion, the despotic ambition, the infuriating spouse, the scent of a new lover's pubic hair. How experience was transformed into words on a page would always be the mystery of writing, the thing that happened behind my father's closed study door. If there was fallout, if a wife, friend, or even a child—*me*—was hurt, exposed, or sacrificed, it was the cost that any and all meaningful work had to pay.

To know the writer *and* the book, then, was to experience reading in many dimensions, to be fully alive and welcoming to all those subliminal and overt vibrations, implicit and buried parallels, to join the imagined and the real so the words rose up on the page and took shape and breath. Uncoupling the writer and the work was not something I was urged or had any desire to do. I still don't. It is more compelling to see how the real and the imagined coil endlessly around each other, their friction creating the work—something I encounter as I write about my father today. The novelist and his silk-shirted wife at the party were evidence of everything that a piece of writing, humming with energy, can give life to: unsettled business, longing, history, shame, pleasure, a million contradictions, the stories we tell to and about ourselves, the ones that trap us, the ones we bury, the ones we bring to life. Remind me to never become a writer, I told myself then.

When I was fourteen, my father gave me Henry Roth's *Call It Sleep* to read. I was so struck by a single passage that I copied it out by hand on lined notebook paper and slipped it under his study door. (This was as close to writing anything myself as I dared to go.) I was uncertain enough about how or even if he'd respond that I also imagined the piece of paper, delivered without ownership or explanation, had just floated down from the sky.

> He blinked, dropped his eyes and looked about him.
> Quiet. Odor of ashes, the cold subterranean breath of chimneys. (—Even up here cellar follows, but only a little bit) And about were roof-tops, tarred and red and sunlit and red, roof-tops to the scarred horizon . . .
> Quiet. Sunlight on brow and far off plating the sides of spires and water-towers and chimney pots and the golden cliffs of the streets. To the east bridge, fragile in powdery light.
> —Gee! Alone . . . Aint so scared.

My father invited me into his study that evening where he sat at his desk and I squeezed next to Olive, the sleeping beagle, in the armchair. It was June, and with the warmer days, Richard, the mysteriously large and terrifying man-boy who lived across the street with his hired keepers and his mother, had started his rhythmic shrieking. The sound was the backdrop to our looking together at the passage that still today seems to roil with the images I had always imagined constituted my father's childhood: a skinny Jewish kid wandering fearlessly and full of fear, unsupervised through the streets of Manhattan, coins in his pockets. I pictured the roofs and gables of Belvedere Castle in Central Park, the American Museum of Natural History, the Dakota—all buildings my father had loved as a kid and talked about with longing. We discussed particular words—*sowed*, *spores*, *scarred*—and the idea that there can be both pleasure and pain in being alone, that contradictions contain sparks you might try to capture for their energy.

"Cold subterranean breath of chimneys," he said.

"Powdery light," I said.

"Scarred horizon," he said.

I might have asked my father, as we waited for the next round of shrieks to subside, Was this what it was like for you? Alone, but—gee!—Ain't so scared? Is this why you gave me the book to read?

But I didn't ask, and he didn't offer or wonder out loud what I was after when I'd copied the passage and given it to him. I thought of the line I hadn't included that struck me hard enough to still remember it: "His father was so silent and so remote that he felt as though he was alone even at his side." I felt alone with my father, always nervous with him, even as we talked, because it wasn't really *us* we were discussing. We were talking plenty, but it was about how stories are told, about writing and reading, about invented people in imagined settings.

I couldn't find the nerve to reveal what was also on my mind that evening: that sixteen-year-old Susanna had just moved into a boyfriend's house because she couldn't get along with my mother; that Polly seemed to prefer animals over people and rarely spoke; that my grandparents' house had recently been broken into, and they'd woken in the middle of the night to find two men at the foot of their bed pointing guns at their heads; or even, in that moment, Richard's unignorable screams filling the space between us, and whether they were anguish or pleasure or something else entirely in his disordered brain. Our discussions about a piece of writing, never his or, later, mine—something we would do forever in lieu of a different kind of honesty—created its own useful fiction of what we were really talking about: the loneliness I had sensed in the passage I had begun to feel myself and was worried would stick with me forever. It was magnified by my inability to talk about it then and would eventually find its way into everything I wrote.

"Writing and reading literary fiction and poetry are activities almost too intimate to talk about," Russell Banks said. Decades later, when Joe was in the hospital in the weeks before he died, I had gone to the bookstore to buy him Edward St. Aubyn's *The Patrick Melrose Novels*, which I was also reading. He placed the book next to the sickly pink plastic water jug, the chocolates he had no taste for anymore, his glasses, his pad and pens, his hearing aids in a little dish. The next time I visited, we admitted to rationing our reading because we didn't want the book to end. His lungs were failing, he wore a nasal cannula, and his breathing sounded like rough surf over small stones.

To offer someone a book chosen above all others is to say, I know what moves you, here is what moves me, read this and we'll be moved together. Reading is how we'll get to know each other and ourselves. When he was in the hospital, we had both teased out the pleasure of that particular novel, one filled with harrowing detail and cruelty, and all the light of their small, fleeting easings, as if in reading it, in inhabiting a different and still difficult world, we could together draw out the time left.

Two years after he died, and finally ready to read it, I pulled my father's Twain biography from the shelf on the second floor of the house I'd lived in for nearly thirty years. I could have chosen any of his other biographies—Lincoln Steffens, or Walt Whitman, or even his last book, *When the Astors Owned New York*—but *Mr. Clemens and Mark Twain* was where he first and most purely experienced the intimate connection a biographer has to his subject. Because this was his initial stab at the form—at any book—he was most open to awe, surprise, and falling in love and to experiencing how a man, a story, and a myth develop in a writer's mind. I wanted to experience this as I read his book, as well as how my father's life, of which so much was unknown to me, might also begin to reveal itself to me through his authorial presence and his deeply sensitive portrait and understanding of Twain.

On top of the bookshelf was a photograph of him steering a small motorboat across Lake Winnipesaukee, taken a few years after the Twain book was published to great acclaim and his career was off to an explosive start. His expression reflects the water and wind and all the things that his life now held and promised, things he could never have imagined.

"Deceased writers are dead and non dead," Janna Malamud writes in *My Father Is a Book*. "The flesh rots and leaves behind the words . . . You read a page, and it is as if you have found some still animate piece of them broken off from the rest and in motion."

I cracked the book's spine, stiff and noisy after so many decades untouched, ready for my father to be set in motion by my first reading of his words.

Three

Coming Into Life

•

"[Twain] seemed to run on nervous energy flogged by ambition, restlessness, the need for money, and, above all, an indecision about who he was and what he wanted to be."

"This biography begins when its subject is already thirty-one," my father types, this first line of the preface of his first book. He begins the book when he is *already* thirty-four, only a few years older than the Twain of his opening page. I imagine him on this fall morning in 1959, in his study on the first floor of the big house on Francis Avenue, also known as Professors Row, sun falling on his hands that hover over the typewriter (he's a two-fingered typist, as I am). He leans back in his chair and allows himself to believe in this moment of grace. He's not sure how he knew where to start, but warmth travels up his arms to his chest and he is sure that this is what it feels like when certainty and risk collide. He is half terrified. I lean back in my chair too, also just beginning this story, although today I am almost twice as old as my impossibly young father.

I considered beginning this chapter with my father's birth in New York City in 1925, to Tobias Kaplan and Anna Rudman Kaplan, their second son after Howard, who was nine years older. Instead I begin with this morning at his desk, because he has guided me to begin where the subject feels himself coming into life—and I see my father coming to life the instant he writes that first line. He would like silence in this moment, but what he hears instead is his new baby—that's me, born a few months earlier—crying. Inconsolable, again. It sounds as if I'm just on the other side of the closed door and that my demands to be let in are seeping through the cracks. I am still on the other side of that door, but today I'm cracking it open to see what happens inside.

My father said he'd never thought about having kids, not once before getting married, had never even held a baby, and now there were two of them under his stately slate roof. On this morning, he imagines he should feel more for this new squawking daughter they've given the old New England name of Hester, middle name Margaret in case she wants something more ordinary later on, and that he should be able to picture who she'll grow up to be, but he can't. I'm a toothless infant, my eyes barely open, and yet our relationship already stumbles and makes him feel too much might be asked of him. My infant demands are simple; I just want him to soothe me, pick me up, or put me in the baby carriage and take me out for a walk in the Cambridge air, but he wants to get back to writing this book, and anyway, what does he know about how to console? He's always had to be his own consolation.

This hour when the infant and her toddler sister are supposed to be napping is also supposed to be his wife Annie's writing time and now she'll have to put her novel down—it will be the first of eight that she'll publish—and tend to the kids. They never discussed this domestic arrangement, just as they never discussed that he would claim this elegant study while she was, and would remain, a writing nomad in the house, the overflowing laundry basket somehow always within view of her desk until my sisters and I leave the house for good. It was simply assumed; in addition to being the man, he's also the one with the book contract. Other men leave to go to work and return later, even if it's long after the children have been put to bed, but he's chosen to work at home and will for the rest of his life, so he'll have to get better at tuning out the noise and need and making his study seem as unreachable as the moon. He will learn to keep the door shut, to bar entrance, to make his babies, his children, his teenagers, his daughters grown into women with children of their own understand they aren't welcome inside and will have to swallow their needs—for him, and then for themselves. He doesn't imagine how this will confuse and sadden them, or how they will begin to talk to each other—only when their own children have left and this story I'm writing starts to take shape—about how he was there and not there at the same time but always present with his work.

But that's many years away still, and on this day, he'll simply get on with the demands of the project, minute by minute and hour by hour, and sand down the distractions until they are smooth. It helps to remind himself that only a few months earlier he had sent his book proposal and outline entitled *A Narrative Biography of Mark Twain in the Gilded Age (1867–1910)* to his mentor and former boss Max Schuster, president of Simon & Schuster. After my father's death, I found the nine onionskin pages he'd preserved in a folder, draft after draft, each with a tiny but critical correction, evidence of his fastidiousness and anxiety at sending the thing off. It had finally gone by airmail to Vienna where Schuster was vacationing. I was born five days later at Columbia's Physician and Surgeon's Hospital in New York while my father was still waiting, hands shaking and skin on itchy fire, for news about what he'd placed all his bets on.

I was six days old when word from Schuster came in a telegram on June 6, 1959:

ATTENTION KAPLAN MARK TWAIN PROJECT ABSOLUTELY MAGNIFICENT BOTH IN FORM AND SUBSTANCE WILL DISCUSS FULL IMPLICATIONS AND ASSIGNMENT OF YOUR RESPONSIBILITIES ON RETURN RESPECT YOUR CREATIVE DEDICATION CONGRATULATIONS ON BABY AFFECTIONATELY.

Even his daydreams, the ones he stockpiles and keeps to himself, had not managed to come up with a scenario quite as good as this one. It's like something out of a movie, pure fantasy of how it happens for writers, how writers still fantasize it will play out for them. Weeks after that telegram arrived, he gave up a promising career as an editor at Simon & Schuster, and he and my mother left Manhattan where they'd both lived their whole lives. They bought the house on Francis Avenue, and with two babies in tow, moved to Cambridge for this amorphous thing he imagined his future might be.

Now in this hour of the first words of his first book, his cat Eloise, also disturbed by the infant's clamor, rises with an arched back and weaves her way between the papers and books and index cards, threatening to topple everything with her nervous tail. My father thinks of making a grab for her, but instead admires her calico expertise in navigating the maze of information and ideas. (If only he were so adept.)

He rereads his first line, aware of how much strange power is in it. But part of him wonders if he should just start instead at Twain's birth in a cabin in 1835; it's what other biographers would do. It would be the safer thing. Does he go with instinct or with caution?

Malamud, who won the National Book Award in 1967, the same year my father did for the Twain biography, wrote in *Dubin's Lives*, a novel about a biographer struggling to make sense of his subject's life, "Beginnings may be more effective independent of strict chronology—where the dominant action of the life starts, the moment of insight, cohesion, decision. You can search that out or perhaps define a moment as a beginning and let what follows prove it."

"I like to think that he had in mind two biographies of mine that had begun midway or toward the end of their subjects' lives," Joe wrote, recalling his long walks with Malamud and their discussions about writing. Disarmingly modest, my father hedges against presumption, but he delights in knowing that in starting where he did, he defined a new kind of beginning for his subject and let what followed prove it. For today, he goes with instinct, the one line is a start, and Jesus Christ, it's exhilarating!

He doesn't have any clue about how many more years he has to go on this project, how every day he'll have to build up his muscle of discipline and stay at his desk if he's going to realize his ambition. He's already been researching and reading and thinking for what seems like a very long time, probably his entire life, from bookish little boy to bookish young man, always thinking about stories and adventures and imagining what it would feel like to be someone else.

He adores the clean light in his new study. He misses the pace and the cool shaded streets of Manhattan, the views from the apartment, the parties, the chance to eat an egg salad sandwich at a coffee shop counter all alone, the romantic, childless freedom when it got dark, but only a little today. Twain had said of his Nook Farm home in Hartford, "Our house was not an unsentient matter—it had a heart and soul, it was of us, and we were in its confidence, and lived in its grace and in the peace of its benediction," and today as my father hears Annie come downstairs with the two children, he takes note of how solid and protective the fifty-year-old house feels around them. It has three floors, thirteen rooms, six tiled fireplaces, yards of crown molding, pocket doors, faceted glass doorknobs, carved newel posts, the bullnose step of a wide and winding staircase, four Ionic columns holding up a front entrance. (It also has a labyrinthine and dank basement with a nonfunctioning toilet, a stone laundry sink, and closets full of my nightmares of kidnappings and torture.) This is a house for adults, and on most days he feels too young and green to own such a place; he and Annie are pretend residents, fumbling their way through how a boiler and a bathtub work. For now, despite the large neighboring houses, he appreciates the lack of material ostentation on the street: the cars are old, the loafers down at the heel, the ties faded, the women's gold earrings small and discreet. What matters here is the mind, originality, and industry, three things he already possesses. He is only very distantly aware of how much work and money a house like this might turn out to demand. He can't imagine how the roof will leak someday when he's written many books and firmly settled into middle age, the windows will refuse to shut, the pipes will squawk, the weeds will tower.

He can't imagine how his children, those two babies he hears and another to come in three years, will increasingly become strangers to him, slam doors, have boys spend the night in their beds, get drunk in the kitchen, run unsupervised through Cambridge, grow tall pot plants outside his window, and entertain fantasies of one day living in houses with no books. He will see one become a high school dean and soccer coach, another a dog trainer and real estate broker, another who will eventually write about him (and marry another writer). He will watch them have children, get divorced, grow older, suffer disappointment and setbacks, and yet still not find a capacity to bear their upset and missteps. They will always wonder why he was unable to apply to them the same curiosity and deeply sensitive insight he brought to understanding and writing about his subjects. He will love them, but he won't ever be able to say this out loud. Those words will not come from his mouth, not even to the grand-children, not even to my son Alexander, who at two will crawl onto his lap, stroke his face, and ask to be read to.

On this morning, he also has no idea how celebrated, ad-mired, and awarded he'll become with the book's publication and how it will set a standard for Twain scholarship and for biography. He doesn't know that he'll be considered an in-novator in the art of literary biography, even still today, in part because of this very beginning, or how the form will consume him for decades. He can't imagine that a review in the *The New York Times*, which he unfolds and refolds with sober precision every morning (it is a crime of disrespect to not refold for the next reader, I will learn early on), will soon say, "Not in years has there been a biography in which the complexities of human character have been exposed with such perceptiveness, with such a grasp of their contradictory nature, with such ability to keep each strand clear and yet make it contribute to the overall fabric."

He doesn't know that he won't fail, but what he already grasps about this undertaking is that at every moment the hard, soul-raking work to find the right means to translate insight, emotion, and another man's experience and shifting self into words and narrative on the page will require him to enter a state of being that is entirely removed from the man he is when he steps out of this room.

What he feels acutely on this day of the first line is that he's a novice, possibly a fraud, despite the encouragement, the book contract, his experience as an editor, his teeth-chattering ambition, and the modest advance. He's sharp, quick-witted, curious, and has read everything, but he has no obvious talent or accomplishments to show for himself, certainly not in writing biography or any other kind of book, for that matter. Who the hell does he think he is to take on such a big-league and iconic subject as Mark Twain? There are scholars for that, and he is definitely not one of them. (His obituary in *The Boston Globe* will call him "an unaffiliated man of letters.") He fears that the experts and academics and historians and writers, the *real* writers, the ones he admires and wants so much to admire him, will box him out, look down their noses, laugh at his pretensions and nerve, and ask, who is this gangly upstart, this graduate school dropout, this shy, stuttering, scratching nobody? But he isn't going to back down. Finding his own unorthodox way is not a terrible thing, and he's used to it, he's good at it. Maybe he is arrogant or just smug. In his quiet pose of observation that he presents to the world, he has been accused of being both. But he is neither.

He scratches his forearms with great energy. He reaches around with a ruler to scratch his back. To answer the despotic itch feels almost worth the suffering it first requires, and his relief as he rakes his skin allows his mind to open and consider the possibility that he might actually have something new to say about Twain, and a new way to say it. And with this first line, which he feels is the right one, he already sees how he can bring the material to life. Expectation and suspense are his engines, and the opposing forces of avalanches and bulwarks are his fuel.

He believes he might be able to write a good book. This is his *job* now, even if no one understands what he's up to, even if he doesn't leave the house to get there. He is comforted by the routine he has established and will keep for more than fifty years, and by what he already knows and has probably always known about writing: it is word after word after word, grinding, not spectacular. The end is so far away, and he has so much work to do to get there, but his new life—and mine when I finally read that very first line so many decades later—depends on it.

Every spring, my father cut giant plumes of lilacs that tapped at his study windows and placed them in vases around the house. One afternoon during the time he was working on *Walt Whitman: A Life*, published in 1980, also a National Book Award Winner for Biography, I caught him with his face buried in the blooms. I thought he was crying—all those tears for his parents eventually had to come out, I was certain, and I'd never seen him cry except when the dog died. Only fiction allows me to imagine what had moved him that day; he was thinking about Whitman, who described the flowers in the dooryard with their heart-shaped leaves of rich green, or about loss and returning spring, or about his mother, whom he remembered so little about beyond that she adored lilacs. (It was the one thing he'd told me about her. My own love for lilacs is boundless as a result.)

"A biography is a tool for imagining another person, to be used with other tools," Louis Menand wrote. Details of the past, like my father's face in the blooms, appear to me now as the bones and seeds of this story I will tell about him. They are how he begins to take shape, how I choose to understand the flow and connection of experience, how his many presentations of self, the private and the public, start to come alive for me. The path of reconstruction is lit by my imagination, while what I've left out or recast suggest many versions of the truth, the elasticity of memory and the driving desire to create sense and meaning. Invention of a life in biography, as in fiction, is a wonder—as well as what my father called "only a plausible, inevitably idiosyncratic surmise and reconstruction."

I am no scholar or even student of Mark Twain. I only know *how* my father wrote about the man, and where and how he recognized the bones and seeds of Twain's story give me insight into him, just as what I recognize in his story gives me insight into myself. I don't pretend detachment or claim the fact-work or thoroughness of the biographer—especially not my father, whose research and knowledge of American history, culture, and literature was exhaustive. My attempt to know him through what he wrote about Twain is cheating and fair play, an affront to those who believe a writer's life is not the same thing as his words, should not even be considered in the same breath, who believe biography is a kind of theft. What I am doing is arrogant, a romantic's view, a trespass, an autopsy done with contaminated instruments.

There is the sound of my father's voice on the page, his eye and ear for pattern and contradiction, the way he massages and pulls at the heart, how he reads and understands the words of others. There is his writing to savor and explore and learn from, the structure, the language, and the art of telling a good story that is also his taste for rhythm, word play, melody, humor, color, image, and impression—what is finally, most profoundly *him*. When I read that he had told an interviewer how "in a purely metaphorical sense, [the biographer] develops the power of life and death over the people you write about," I felt him reach into the future to remind me of the responsibility I've taken on. Through my writing about his life, and mine with him, he is fully revived for me.

My father described Whitman's feeling about his "random autobiography," *Specimen Days*: "Perhaps thinking of his own history as well, [Whitman] had warned his readers that 'the real war will never get into the books . . . will never be written—perhaps must not and should not be.' "

What I am doing would have made Joe uncomfortable, even angry. I can imagine the flush of his face, how he'd avert his gaze and make some joke, then get serious and explain that his privacy, his real war, was his alone. "Mind your own beeswax," he'd say, shake his head, turn red in the face, stutter. "I mean it." He might say my life risks becoming dangerously mixed up with his, that I've riskily mixed up his with Twain's, and that I've failed to preserve what he called "a certain empathetic distance."

If he'd read "The Biographer," he might suggest that I stop there, that there was nothing more I need to know, and fiction had done the job. But he'd eventually accept too that there is much more for me to discover about him and myself through writing his story, and that he is fair game for me because it's what he'd left me to do. He might admit that it's also what he taught me to do, his gift to me, so I might find my own way and place at this late date, and that the dead don't get to choose who digs into their life.

"Diffidently and erratically, already past the age when others have chosen their vocation, [Twain] was beginning to choose his," he writes on another morning. There's that word *already* again, carrying with it the same whiff of impatience he feels about his own tempo and foot-dragging in getting to this moment. I want to whisper to him from the future that he has plenty of time; I want the same whisper to reach me today. What took me so long to get to this story when it's the one that has always compelled me, the one that already makes me feel newly alive?

When he writes about Twain facing east to begin his life as America's Greatest Writer, he feels how far away the real world can seem when he's in his study thinking about another life in another time. He understands he has a responsibility to be of the moment, that no art can seal itself off from real life, and that this distancing from the present is a form of luxury that piques his lifelong sense of guilt. Money left to him by his father, a man whose success in creating the Dexter Shirt Company allowed that his own two sons shouldn't grow up to make schmattes like he had, along with a rich father-in-law, is responsible for all this freedom and buffeting, these fine rooms, this leafy street, these babies and ambitious wife, and this crazy determination to write a book.

Antsy, he stands and gazes up and down Francis Avenue, a short walk to Harvard Yard where he'd spent his undergraduate and aborted graduate school years. He imagines his neighbors, those experts, scholars, academics, writers, thinkers, the men who have barely acknowledged him since he moved in and who will probably never tender an invitation or start a conversation, working at their own desks.

He is already familiar with how Cambridge is a hard place to belong, a mean city, competition and exclusion delivered in a quietly devastating fashion, and he assumes that he will never really be part of this exclusive street that exists not in the shadow of Harvard, but in its bullying graces. He might be known as the man who tried and failed amid all these men who tried and succeeded.

He spots three of these guys talking on the sidewalk near the linden tree. He'll eventually discover that "What are you working on?" is always their opening gambit. A few times he'll answer "chicken paprikash" or "feeding the dog," pretending he doesn't understand their real question: *What is your worth today?* They won't be amused, but making fun of their self-seriousness will remain one of his great pleasures. Like Twain, my father "wanted to belong, but he also wanted to laugh from the outside." He knows that if he were to step outside and join the trio, he'd be gripped by his shyness and stutter, an impediment Twain himself regarded as an infirmity akin to his own drawl. He marvels at their certainty of belonging, even if it's something he's not sure he wants for himself, and can't imagine that these are the same people— Howard Mumford Jones, Arthur Schlesinger Jr., and John

Kenneth Galbraith—whose praise will appear on the back of the paperback edition of *Mr. Clemens and Mark Twain* in a few years.

Stop wasting time, he scolds himself, turning away from the men who are old enough to be his many fathers. There will never be enough of it. But time is not the problem, we both know, it's fear that holds the writer back, and only when I read his obituary in *The New York Times* do I learn just how scared he was writing the book. "I would wake up at 2:00 or 3:00 in the morning, terrified, and ask myself, 'What have I done?'"

He recalls what he wrote in his book proposal: "Like no other major American writer, Twain flung himself into his time. The frontiers of his experience as writer and man of his age never closed . . . In telling the story of his triumphs and frustrations, his ambitions and conflicts, [the biography] will also reveal something about the terms of existence for the good life and for the creative life in late 19th century America."

I also feel flung, he thinks, *and these are the terms of existence for my good and creative life.* He takes in his own frontier again, even if it is only this tree-lined street with the asphalt that turns crimson in the rain. When later he writes that Twain at work in his octagonal study at Quarry Farm in Elmira, New York, "could see city and countryside, storms sweeping down the valley, flashes of lightning over the distant blue hills. Everything lay below the study and beyond," he remembers this day he stood at the window and believed that his vista was no less spectacular, everything waiting for him beyond the glass.

"A few words to explain this abruptness may be in order," my father wrote, acknowledging his own breathless but confident leap from Twain's childhood to his adulthood in that brave and startling first line. "Samuel Clemens' early years . . . were both his basic endowment in raw experience and his favorite subject . . . But the central drama of his mature literary life was his discovery of the usable past. He began to make this discovery in his early and middle thirties—a classic watershed age for self-redefinition—as he explored the literary and psychological options of a new, created identity called Mark Twain." It was his choice of the word *redefinition* rather than *definition* that reflected his own experience that the journey to becoming oneself begins with the reshaping of who you had once been.

That morning in 1959, in his study in Cambridge, my father was just beginning to sense that his own early years of profound and disorienting loss might be usable too for its insight into the creation of identity. His early years were his basic endowment in raw material that shaped his sensibility and attraction to biography, and once he'd found the form, it was a revelation that allowed him to bring to the understanding of another person every bit of experience and understanding from his own life.

"The imaginative and structural use of what he had known,

seen, and been" was for Twain, as it was for Joe, a source of energy, a hard nugget wrapped in tissue paper giving off the heat he needed to write. Many years after the biography was published, seeing the symmetry between his life and Twain's, my father wrote that in one's midthirties, "one either made a decisive change then or resigned oneself to continuing on the same path." Today his decision to elide Twain's early years suggests to me, more crudely than he might approve of, the elision of his own early years that defined him and yet left him without a solid sense of who he might become.

"Every man is a moon and has a dark side which he never shows to anybody," Twain had said, my father adding that this "tacitly suggest[ed] that this dark side might be hidden from himself as well." He'd written that Twain acknowledged that "introspection and self-analysis were not his strong suit." They were not my father's strong suit either, but his sensitivity to the psyches and inner lives of his subjects was the gift allowing him to write with compassion and conviction. He believed that as a form, biography "shapes experience, narrative, and character, the way we look at history, and other people." It is through his weaving together experience, art, and accidents of another man's existence that I see him shedding light not only on the mysterious process of the writer, but on the private man he believed was the "most richly endowed natural talent in American history."

Could he have known that he also began an illumination of his hidden self and his own shadowed moon for me when he wrote his first biography?

"The question for a good biographer," he wrote, "is not

why but how: how it felt for the subject of the biography to live his life." He spent his career uncovering how others navigated storms to find their place in the world, and in constructing the narrative of another's life, my father was always constructing and navigating his own. Like Twain, "his richest choices as man and writer came from deep imperatives of his sensibility . . . these choices take on a special dignity both because they were inescapable and because they were evolved in such adversity."

It was his own history that made him a biographer. As an orphan, he had to write his own story. ("Whether I shall turn out to be the hero of my own life, or whether that station will be held by anybody else, these pages must show," David Copperfield, another abandoned boy, says.) It was a wayward process, but he had no choice if he was going to thrive, and he was fiction writer, protagonist, and autobiographer at the same time. As I write about him, I am biographer informed by discovery, fiction writer freed by invention, and protagonist. I am compelled by the demands of narrative to tell the story of a life, why and how it happened, and how it felt to live that life.

But be careful, my father might caution me even now; *you can't bend the facts of a person's life in order to write the story you want.* He might also warn me of the risk of overidentification, of conjecture, of asking questions that lead only to the clarity and satisfaction I hope for, of becoming a joint tenant in the writing of his life.

As an undergraduate, he had written a few short stories but had struggled with how to handle the problem of the ego, the self, and the first person in fiction; biography as a form had freed him to bring everything he knew about life to the understanding of another man. I am not stymied by my own point of view or the form this work takes: I am his daughter, and my story of him is neither right nor wrong, wholly true nor fully false. What I write is only one version of the story—all children are their parents' biographers—but it is mine.

Four

His Other Family

•

"When I find a well-drawn character in fiction or biography . . . I generally take a warm personal interest in him, for the reason that I have known him before—met him on the river."

On the very rare occasion that my father's study door was open and I was invited in, he tracked my movements. He was rarely unkind, and often playful, but he was uncomfortable with me in there. Twain wrote about "my double, my partner in duality, the other and wholly independent personage who resides in me." Even as a child I was looking for my father's double, the other self who lived more fully in the study, so when I was let in, I had to move fast.

Inside, I examined the fireplace with its silky black hearth cold under my bare feet and its surround of glazed green tiles, its mantelpiece crowded with items of mysterious significance I wanted to decode: a photograph he had taken of my mother, pre-children, nude in a bathtub, half covered by a washcloth; a silver salt cellar shaped like a wheelbarrow; a tiny green glass lady's slipper on a cube of granite; a porcelain box that was replica of a Palladian villa, its roof a lid hiding treasures inside. It was an irresistible collection of objects, fragile, exotic, and not meant for me. The naked picture of my mother was proof enough that I shouldn't even cast my eyes there and that this room held a life that was entirely separate from my own. Surprisingly, my father's study was always open during their many parties like a museum exhibit of "the writer at work" minus the velvet ropes. I don't know what visitors to the study made of the intimacy displayed in that photo of my mother when they reverently entered the room. If her bare breasts and tilted head made them uncomfortable, for my parents this only confirmed the erotic mythology of their partnership.

Because my father's past involved an intensity of experience I struggled to imagine, I was particularly drawn to the objects he'd had as a kid—foreign coins, inkless fountain pens, rusted trinkets from his shrouded past. (Just the words *when I was a boy*, my father suggested, could start up Twain's writing engine.) I sensed that when he looked at these objects of a previous life, they started up his own engine he needed to remember and to write. There was a heavy model car, about eight inches long, pewter gray, that could be wound by a small key attached to a red ribbon and made to cross the length of his study floor. At one time, I was sure that the car was a model of the one that had taken King Edward and Wallis Simpson away from Buckingham Palace. Other times I thought it was a replica of the one Hitler had ridden, or Charles Lindbergh after his baby had been kidnapped, these waywardly gathered historical markers part of my attempt to ground and animate my father's childhood in place, time, and texture.

The walking stick in the corner had belonged to his father. I never saw him touch it, skeletal like some femur dug up from a grave. I knew better than to put my hands on it. On his desk, books were held open by the paperweight I'd made for his birthday by wrapping a red brick in batting and flowery Marimekko fabric, the 1970s version of Twain's "brickbats." Colored index cards, covered with his scratchy handwriting, rose in careful piles. There was his gold pencil, the lead still connected to the last word he'd written on the yellow pad before I intruded.

The framed photograph of a shirtless Mark Twain—all bushy mustache, thick chest hair, and nipples—made me uncomfortable in a way I didn't understand. He was, after all, not just some random guy on the beach. It was as though I'd opened my parents' bedroom door to find him in the sheets with them. Tightly packed bookshelves lined three walls of the room. Books, I'd been taught, were never to be pushed to the back of a shelf; spines were to be lined up an inch from the front edge. If I took a book from the shelf, I was careful to put it back exactly where it had been. There were volumes by and about Mark Twain, Lincoln Steffens, and Walt Whitman, but also Freud and Thoreau, Nabokov and Gandhi, Hemingway and Pound, Jews in New York in the 1930s, the Civil War, movies, atlases, dictionaries, *Bartlett's Familiar Quotations*, and long expanses of reference books. Of particular interest to me were the *Pictorial Atlas of Skin Diseases* (a chancred penis made me wince, erotic and sickening), the book of dirty limericks, and the *Dictionary of American Slang*, because it was full of bad words I slung around like a pro. There was the copy of *The Adventures of Huckleberry Finn* with the titillating front etching my father had shown me: "An engraver, whose identity was never discovered . . . made a last-minute addition to the printing plate of Kemble's picture of old Silas Phelps," he had written. "In the mischievous tradition of graffiti he drew in a male sex organ, and what was originally a pleasant scene shared by an appreciative Aunt Sally asking, 'Who do you reckon it is?' suddenly became a flagrant case of indecent exposure."

The air in the study was different from the rest of the house, alive with webs of ideas and words and things I couldn't touch. Everything was solid, but everything was fragile and easy to shatter, like a memory, or a dream, or a half-written sentence. Easy to understand, then: Do. Not. Enter. This. Hester. Means. You.

Which meant, of course, that it was exactly where I wanted to be. Even the thought of a single step into the room when he wasn't there was an act cloaked in thrill, transgression, and the expectation that I might discover something that justified the risk. But the one time I trespassed, I was too brave and too careless, and my presence in the room was a disaster; I'd scattered his index cards across the floor and panicked to pick them up in their right order. He might fix what I'd broken, but I knew his book would never be the same. That he never acknowledged what I'd done did not lessen my shame then— or now.

During my early childhood, the entirety of which my father seemed to be writing the Twain book, I believed that my father and Twain were related in a million ways. More than that, I knew that on some other plane of existence they were the same person. This certainty hasn't dimmed over the years, and when I look again at a photo of Twain and his family, I'm still struck by the feeling that I'm gazing at my father's other family.

On a porch shaded by foliage, Twain's wife, Livy, looks dotingly on the youngest of three daughters, the oldest looks at the camera as though she's just beginning to wake up to the idea of self-presentation and independence, and the middle child, in a pleated skirt, rests shyly against her father's side, hoping not to be seen, hoping to be protected. That's me, and those are my sisters already assuming our identities and places within the family. Twain's three-piece suit fits him nicely, and his legs crossed at the ankles give him a casual and optimistic arrogance, one that hides his self-doubt and darkness, his passion for ruinous moneymaking schemes, his impatience. Twain and my father, both writers, are the providers, the stars, and the center of all this female life.

There were other convergences. We also had a wooden porch cascaded with grape vines and shaded by trees. Twain loved cats and so did my father. Twain had suffered the early loss of his father, just as my father had. This made them different from other people, gave them membership into a secret society. (When I met my husband, he told me that people who had lost a parent early—as he had—could always detect each other in a crowded room because they emitted a different frequency.)

Both men had searing wits, both delighted in making other people laugh, often in discomfort. Both gazed somewhere into the distance in photographs, their minds always on their work. These shared details confirmed for me then that a biographer—that every writer, I'd come later to understand when I began to put characters on a page—had to possess a mystical and ordained link to his subject, and that some spiritual twinning and affinity existed even before the first word had been written. Without parents, my father was a hereditary free agent who could adopt Twain as his father, guide, or model and bring him back to life on the page. Like Twain, my father "was in part the father as well as the child of the circumstances that made him." Before he put Twain's story into words, he knew it in his own bones and blood because a person couldn't and wouldn't write a biography without such profound familiarity.

My father wrote of Twain's work habits that "he worked steadily through the day until dinnertime . . . The writer Mark Twain worked in the same solitary, untouchable splendor as Sam Clemens the pilot. He was isolated—from Livy, children, servants, the entire domestic context. He was 'remote from all noise.'"

Isolated. Remote. These words stun me when I encounter them on the first read of my father's book because they are the same ones I've always used to describe him. "A solitary and untouchable splendor": this is what he wanted, too, even as he worked in the house. "The genius works in a dazzling darkness of his own which normal modes of explanation hardly penetrate," my father wrote. The resonance with how he described Twain's writing habits has the shock of the most intimate recognition, as though I'm standing outside my father's study door again.

When Joe emerged from writing at the end of the day to have a gin and tonic, cook, play a round of casino at the kitchen table, tease and gossip and read to me and my sisters as we ate dinner, his presence often felt provisional and precarious. At any minute, provoked by nothing I could discern, he might announce that he needed to "write something down" and disappear again into his study, evidence that there was another, more urgent, more real life going on in there and in his head. My sisters and I treated him with the deference afforded to a visitor and learned not to blink at this, but I felt his leavings as a thousand abandonments. The three of us knew how much our labile biology made him uneasy, how our shoes left under the table, our scented shampoos, moods, Day-Glo posters taped and ruinous to old walls, our carelessness with a book could distress him to the point of silent fury and flight. At the first note of conflict or a raised voice, of which there was plenty in this house of females—even the dog was a girl, he would complain—he began to melt and flutter and appear deeply pained, imploring us in a voice barely above a stuttering whisper to calm down.

He would often take walks alone with the dog by the Charles River in the afternoon. He reeked of smoke when he returned, but when I asked, he refused to admit that he'd been smoking even as the opened box of cigarillos poked out of his coat pocket. I pictured him lighting up, blowing smoke out of the side of his mouth, and felt acutely how much he was hidden from me. "Why not just admit it?" I'd press as he fled to his study, when what I really wanted to find out was, "Which is the real you? Which of you loves me?"

Maleness, in addition to genius and literary stature, bestowed on him the unquestioned right of self-protection and withdrawal from trouble. From us. "'O, for a life of don't-give-a-damn in a boardinghouse,' Mark Twain said in some vaguely approximate situation," my father had written to a friend describing the challenges of balancing family life and work one particular summer. When I found this letter after he died, I remembered that summer when I was eight, a bowered path of cherry laurel down to a lake in New Hampshire, a day bed on a screened porch with a book I'd spent my own quarter on that morning at a yard sale because I'd liked its green and gold tooled cover. I pretended to read it and appear bookish and smart, even though I couldn't understand a word of it. In the evening, my parents had cocktails on the grass with another couple, and I had a sensation of knowing I would never forget this moment. When I read my father's letter so many years later describing his "vaguely approximate" longing to be unfettered in those days, I understood that I must have already sensed it in how he looked toward the water, smiling genially. It was the child's awakening to the impermanence of perfection, of any moment, and the beginning of the writer's impulse to recapture it.

When my father wrote that for Twain seclusion was a

matter of "stating the terms of his eventual survival," he had already begun to adopt the same terms and permissions necessary for his own work and survival. When I came across a passage he'd marked many years later in Geoff Dyer's *Out of Sheer Rage*, a book he greatly admired, I detected his sense of vindication about the choices he'd made: "For some writers there has scarcely been any friction between the demands of the life and the demands of the work. John Updike arranged his circumstances to his liking fairly early on and then simply got on with his writing, book after book, day after day."

My father wrote about the extent to which Twain's "life and literary goals were to be victimized by malign and domestic harassments." His use of the word *victimized* suggests his feeling that what robbed Twain—or any writer—of the quiet and detachment he needed to work was a crime. But who was the criminal? Was I? Were we? What my father called malign and domestic harassments, I call life, and for a moment I am thrust back to those times I stood outside his study door seeking company, clarity, comfort, too afraid to not hear "come in." And so, I didn't knock, I never did. Later, when my own kids knocked on my door when I was writing, I always let them in. I soothed and listened and took my hands off the keyboard. I would not be like my father. Still, over their beautiful heads, I watched my words leave the room, the crime complete.

I saw another symmetry in the fact that like Mark Twain, my father had more than one name. "[Mark Twain's] pseudonym put a liberating distance between the humorist, novelist, and satirist, a public figure, and Samuel L. Clemens, householder, family man, and intensely private citizen. But at the same time it is the edgy traffic between these two identities— their opposing pulls and obligations, their 'twainship' and twinship—that make him a rich subject for biography and the psychology of naming," my father wrote in *The Language of Names: What We Call Ourselves and Why It Matters*, published in 1999 and coauthored with my mother.

Some people called my father Justin, many more called him Joe (which is not actually a nickname for Justin), and if they didn't know any better, Joseph. He introduced himself as Justin. My mother called him Joe, Justin, and sometimes, Jojo. Also Just-in-Time, suggesting that my father was heroic and always quick to her rescue. My father's shifting names invite my attempts to understand his own relationship to the various personas attached to them. I know that to be called by the wrong name, as I am so often, is to experience the slipperiness of identity and the battle between the selves.

"Names penetrate the core of our being and are a form of poetry, storytelling, magic, and compressed history," Joe had written. He claimed he was something of an aficionado of names and naming because he was a biographer, but his real knowledge was rooted in his own experience of the struggle between the private and public person, the man inside the study and outside of it.

"In all likelihood Samuel Clemens simply invented the name Mark Twain. It is associated with the river, timeless symbol of the creative unconscious," he wrote. He was skeptical of Twain's claim that he had taken the name as a tribute to an old pilot, suggesting that it had perhaps more to do with how saloon keepers marked drinks on credit. In any case, he was attuned to the significance of what we call ourselves and what we're called by others. *Justin* means fair or just. *Joseph* comes burdened with all its Old Testament weight. But *Joe* is everyone and no one at the same time, nondescript, ordinary: Joe College, Average Joe. A cup of coffee.

The name on his birth certificate was Justin, a name his mother had chosen and his father had hated. After her death, my grandfather had returned to using what had all along been his first name choice for the boy: Joseph. Gone now was the echo of his mother calling *Justin* that must have filled their apartment and my father's dreams. In his place, Joseph was beckoned, a new kid washed of trauma and full of promise and a fresh start, or so his father wanted to believe.

Joe wrote with characteristic distance in *The Language of Names* that after his father's death, "I was left with a double first-name identity. By the time I went to college, I had begun to define the situation in this way. Joseph was the double orphan, alone, afraid, uncertain. Justin was an evolving, more confident, and more competent sort of person, who had begun to see the possibility of finding his way to definition through love and work."

While a double name can mirror a psychic and emotional incongruity, a chosen name can also be a firewall. Although my father claimed to "resent and reject just about everything associated with *Joe*," my sisters and I never called him anything *but* Joe because we weren't allowed to. Never Dad or

Daddy, Papa (which is what Twain's daughters called him), or even the more formal Father. He wouldn't give us an explanation for why we couldn't use the names other children used and other men seemed to happily respond to, beyond the unconvincing fact that they were unoriginal and sappy. It was easy to make him squirm by calling him Daddy, especially in public, but even then, even as a joke, the name was like a burr sitting on my tongue.

To hear everyone else call my father by the same name I did made me feel that I had no special access to him, no special relationship or status, certainly not in the eyes of the world. A parent in a room full of children calling out *Daddy* or *Papa* hears the intimacy not in the name itself but in the tone that belongs only to his child. I was unmoored by having to call him Joe and ashamed of my desire for something so simple yet deemed so pedestrian. *Dad* exists only because his child does; he is defined by his role. *Dad* is unconcerned with who he is beyond that title, and my father chose not to cede his identity, not even for his children. To him, *Dad* suggested age, mortality, and his unfinished business with his own father. And the son without a father is no one's child and no one's parent either. He can just be Joe.

Once, when I was about ten, the mother of a new friend of mine asked if Joe, the person on his way to pick me up, was my stepfather. When I said no, she asked if he was my mother's boyfriend. Her look told me that she suspected some funny business going on. "You should call him Dad, then," she scolded. "Or Daddy, so people don't get confused."

I am not the one who is confused, I thought, bitterly, but I was.

My father knew that a new name could herald a new start. "When [Twain] was twenty-seven, a western journalist writing a travel letter to his paper from Carson City in the Nevada Territory, he described himself as feeling 'very much as if I had just awakened from a long sleep.' He signed the piece, 'Yours, dreamily, Mark Twain.' . . . The first known appearance in print of the most famous pseudonym in American literature signaled a great personal discovery."

A new name was the beginning of the invention of one's own mythology, and in his reclaiming the name *Justin* as the emerging adult, the man who would become the acclaimed biographer, my father also rejected the imposition of identity from any outside force. Also awakened out of a long sleep, he returned himself to the newly born and newly (re)named moment where anything was possible. With Justin, he was a "twice-born man," as he believed Twain was, and the transformative power of a name could set him free to find his own way.

Because I have been so often called by the wrong name—Heather, Esther, Hector, Custard—I am intimate with that moment of fury, erasure, and estrangement from myself that comes from being called by a name that isn't mine. When I began this book, and echoing my father echoing Twain, I began to introduce myself as Hes, simple and whispery, to see what would happen. Every time I hear myself called that, a name I have finally given myself, I feel a brighter, fresher, and truer me recognized.

Later, my father expressed some feeling that *Mr. Clemens and Mark Twain* might have been too crude a title, and that such simple dualities were no longer adequate to explain a man's enigmatic nature. By then he was over eighty, and maybe the years had cooled the squabbles of his own feelings of the divided self. What had initially fascinated him—the subliminal and contradictory forces that drive people, the navigation through ambivalence—might now be a kind of bittersweet notion in the finality of old age when you are left with yourself.

If my father was a reverberation of Twain, his aftershock, his incarnation, his ageless double, then he lived with the other family in that portrait in a fully engaged way he didn't live with us. The three daughters in that picture knew all the things about him—his childhood, his parents, his adventures and fears—that I didn't and am still searching for. He talked to them in a way he didn't to me. He told them he loved them, but he never said it to me. He hugged them when he never hugged me. The child's logic holds stubbornly to the adult; I still feel the hands of this other family pulling him toward them and away from me. My father talked about a "certain symmetry" in his choosing to write about Twain. His choice of words contains the cold beauty of math, but when he looked at that portrait as I do today, I know he must have also felt the hot pull of home.

Five

The Fortune of His Life

•

*" 'I do hope this will be the last season that it will
be necessary for you to lecture,' Livy wrote . . .
She minded the separation as much as he did,
told him that she dreamed about his return, about
stroking his hair and putting her hand in his."*

"I was reminded of what Justin Kaplan, Mark Twain's biographer, called the first rule of biography: 'Shoot the widow,'"
Meryle Secrest wrote. My father's efficient advice suggests
the biographer's inevitably fraught task of extracting information from someone who has her own version of history and
shifting memories to support her intentions. She may give up
the stories freely or fiercely withhold them, distort them by
accident or by design, blunt or sharpen them with her grief
or her loyalty.

My father could not have imagined that someday those
needing to be shot might be both his wife and his daughter.

My mother was his wife for more than five decades, and
asking her to shed light on him can be a sticky venture. One

morning, when I was in the early stages of this book, she and I were in the car on Route 6, a notoriously dangerous road on the outer Cape Cod, where my parents had owned a house and spent their summers since the early 1970s. She was behind the wheel because she insisted. White-haired and steady-handed, she's a remarkably assured driver and enthusiastic verbal road-rager who can't imagine that at ninety-two, her swearing and giving people the finger will ever get her in trouble. She pulled a U-turn across several lanes, a daring move eliciting a gasp from me but only delight from her, so unlike her husband who panicked at even the thought of executing a maneuver like this. With him driving, our destination was often determined by whether or not it involved crossing this highway.

My father's remarkable authorial confidence often seemed at odds with his lack of confidence in other spheres of life and particularly behind the wheel—his fear of driving, of getting lost (imprecise directions infuriated him), running out of gas, having to back up in a crowded parking lot, entrance and exit ramps, navigating the arrivals and departure signs at Logan Airport, traffic circles, being honked at. When he drove, he clutched the wheel with two hands, his shoulders hunched humorlessly, sweat beading on his forehead like a man preparing for disaster.

Hoping my mother might have an explanation, I asked her why she thought Joe was such an uneasy driver.

"That's absolutely not true," she snapped, as though I hadn't been in the back seat all those years. "He was an excellent driver."

Her unsatisfying answer was unsurprising. Despite my pressing her on many fronts, she refused to offer up any psychological speculation about him, even though as a novelist who traffics in just such conjecture, she's adept at it. Revealing her own misgivings about this book, at times she waged a domestic public relations campaign about him that would have made her own father, Edward L. Bernays, double nephew of Sigmund Freud, and the self-appointed inventor of the profession of PR (and author of *Propaganda*, *Crystallizing Public Opinion*, and *The Engineering of Consent*, among other unabashedly virile titles), proud.

"And don't say mean things about my husband," she added. As though he wasn't also my father.

Her blocking of my access to him, intellectually and otherwise, often took the form of intrusions on our time alone together as father and daughter. One Sunday, when I was in my midforties and had already published a couple of books, we were at party when my father pulled me aside into an empty room.

"I read your latest story," he whispered.

Was this finally the moment he'd talk to me about my work? I still wasn't sure I was ready to be so exposed. After all, I hadn't ever mentioned the story or its publication; its path to him was mysterious, though my mother often made a point of seeking out my work as if to suggest she was fully on to me and we were in some kind of competition.

"Why are we whispering?" I whispered back, my heart beating uncertainly.

He glanced at the guests moving around in the other room

and at my mother who had spotted us and was quickly approaching. "Because she made me promise not to talk to you about your work unless she's here, too."

It was a deeply unsettling thing to hear and made me feel that my father and I might never reach each other, in part because of his acquiescence. I don't know what he'd made of my story of a father navigating between his son and the boy's mother, or if he recognized the parallels. Something in it had spurred him enough to want to talk about it, though, but the opportunity passed and never returned.

There are a thousand variations on the theme of a mother blocking a daughter's access to her father, a thousand more about her blocking a father's access to his daughter. (I am fascinated by my mother's underlinings and exclamation points in her copy of Adrienne Rich's *Of Woman Born*: "The cathexis between mother and daughter—essential, distorted, misused—is the great unwritten story.") A new view reveals itself to me when I revisit this moment when my father and I *almost* talked: my father's choice every day, except for this brief and foiled moment, not to step, out of fear of upsetting his marriage, into a sharper light with his daughter. Today I wonder if I had failed to understand that, like me, he'd been waiting all along for me to ask him to read what I'd written.

My parents were fiercely protective of each other and presented a unified front as impenetrable to their children as to the outside world. When I was a child, I thought of their marriage as seamless as the glass orb, an anniversary present from my father, that sat by my mother's side of the bed. When I looked through it, the familiar scene of their gently messy bedroom, the long cluttered upstairs hallway, the closed doors of our bedrooms, the overflowing bookshelves and wheezing humidifier always running to soothe my father's tormented skin, appeared inverted, as if to say that only they could see the view from there. As if to say, the view was only for them.

"We're temperamentally dissimilar in many ways," my mother told an interviewer for *New Woman* in 1989. "He likes solitude; I have to be around people . . . Justin almost never complains when something is bothering him, but everyone within earshot knows about my troubles immediately." When probed for the secret to a long union, she claimed "compromise," and my father "inertia." About marriage, my father also said, "My formula for success, such as we've had it, is patience, humor, and resignation." Like Twain, he "enjoyed and exploited playing the role of a man under his wife's thumb," a position of both equanimity and hostility masquerading as humor and long suffering.

They were known as Anne and Joe or Justin and Anne, the biographer and the novelist, central figures in the area's robust literary scene. It thrilled my mother and embarrassed my father when their names appeared in the *Boston Herald* or *The Boston Globe* announcing new books or attendance at important literary events, along with items about celebrity sightings and professional athletes spotted shopping on Newbury Street. They shared teaching appointments, guest editorships, and interviews and were not unlike many other successful couples in the striving and competitive environment of Cambridge, duos who publicly made little distinction between their professional and personal partnership. I went to school with many of their children who, like me, orbited their parents' sun and accomplishments and understood we were incidental to that universe.

My parents were proud of their marriage and fascinated by how other couples could go so wrong. I listened to them speculate about what could have provoked a friend to chuck a frozen pork chop at her husband's head, leaving him with a bleeding gash that required a trip to the ER. What about the husband who wouldn't allow his painter wife to hang any of her art in the house because, he said, matter-of-factly to her face that it was just "too fucking ugly"?

I devoured their stories about strange arrangements, unusual desires, and searing cruelties: how one man, a well-known economist and part-time poet, had siphoned off money over years until there was nothing left but his note to his wife stating, "and by the way, I never loved you," as the final accounting. I heard about the renowned scientist who, it turned out, had a secret other family; the psychiatrist who screwed his patients while their husbands paid the bills for the fifty-minute sessions; and the writer who moved his mistress into the house and told his wife she was his assistant—a claim no one but her believed.

Holding a map of these stories in my head, I biked past the house on Huron Avenue where I'd heard a professor of American literature was sleeping with her graduate student twenty years her junior; three doors down, her husband slept with their two farting bulldogs. On Craigie Street I imagined the man, who after finding his wife's lover's tie in the glove compartment, had sold their almost new car the same day for $100. When I went to my grandparents', I thought of the woman on their block who had discovered what her husband was up to when she opened up the morning's paper to read about a fire at a downtown hotel. There on the front page was a photograph of the guests who had been evacuated from the burning building, her husband and his lover in matching terry cloth robes among them.

Sometimes there was great tragedy in the stories I heard, and I never turned away from them or their mystery and intensity, even as they scared me. On discovering her husband was having an affair, my sister's friend's mother had killed him, their two young daughters, and the family dog as they slept. In the months after, I often steered my bike to that house, looking for something emanating from it that would explain how and why the mother had decided this was the answer, how certainty gripped her and wouldn't let her go. I wanted to arrive at that instant when she felt the ground under her disappear, her hands went cold, and she remembered some ancient moment when she was a girl and had a first inkling of love's betrayal.

But it was just a small, white house with a FOR SALE sign and a pot of unwatered geraniums by the front door. If I wanted to understand anything, including how a mother could stand at the foot of her children's beds and decide to kill them, I'd have to write that story myself. Looking up to the window shades pulled down to precisely the same level in the bedrooms, I'd have to refill those spaces with the handsome father and those girls I saw every day at school and work backward, imagining life in reverse to discover the beginning that led to the end as the mother, deranged by heartbreak, entered the dark rooms and pulled the trigger.

Two writers in one marriage meant it wasn't always smooth sailing. My mother raged one night at having been introduced at a party as "Mrs. Mark Twain." It was like watching her try to shake out a poison that ran through her body, my father made mute by her distress. Another time she'd been introduced as a "lady novelist," a double whammy of disparagement. Despite her success at publishing novels at a steady pace, her considerable achievements always lived in the shadow of my father's (and her father's) work. The world took him and his writing more seriously because he was a man, because his work was nonfiction, because it involved scholarship and spoke more broadly to history and society, while hers was made-up small stuff like family life, marriage, the kitchen, the bedroom. It was a ranking I didn't question, and one I still have to fend off, even about my own work at times, in part because I know my father bought into it too on some level, though he always claimed otherwise. My mother never stopped pushing against how the world devalued her work, and when my father was invited to lecture or give a reading, she often lobbied him to either secure an invitation for her as well or not accept. The lack of respect she felt could be remedied only by her inclusion, but it seemed to me like a force-fed corrective that my father swallowed out of guilt and a desire above all to avoid conflict.

In 2004, they posed seminaked together for a fundrais-
ing calendar of Cambridge celebrities, or rather my mother
shamed him into doing it. She delighted in baring it all, while
exposure of any kind was excruciating for him. When the calendar arrived, my sisters and I refused to look at it despite my
mother's insistence, and my father hid out in his study. He
was embarrassed and angry, but after all, he had agreed to it,
and maybe it was his giving in to her out of a need to maintain
harmony and her loyalty to him at all costs that he was most
ashamed of.

In the summer of 1971, my mother published an op-ed in
The New York Times titled "Radical Chic on the Cape" about
a summertime benefit party thrown by their friends for the
Harrisburg Defense Fund, complete with an appearance by
Daniel Ellsberg. Written in a breathless present-tense pace, it
exposed what my mother considered performative politics and
the self-important, celebrity-centric fatuousness of her peers.

The social order on the outer Cape was unforgiving, and
her punishment for having published the piece was exclusion
from this particular circle from then on. At first, she seemed
surprised and hurt, as though she didn't understand the most
basic rule all little girls understand from an early age: you
can't make fun of a friend and expect to be invited to her
slumber party. She protected her pride with the writer's last
and worst justification: the piece was published in the *Times*,
so it had to have merit.

My father suffered collateral damage, similarly removed
from that season's social calendar. And though at home and
to friends he would feign confusion about why he had to pay

the price when, in his words, it was his dog who had done the biting, he always defended my mother's decision to write and publish what she wanted. It's impossible to believe that he didn't read and edit drafts of the article before she sent it off. In fact, he was likely the corroborating source of many of the piece's observations because they would have talked about the party at length, over meals and on walks, and arrived at a shared and therefore unimpeachable conclusion. It's harder still to believe that he couldn't have talked her out of publishing it if he'd wanted to and hadn't taken some pleasure in its mocking of pretense.

She fired the gun, but he supplied the bullets.

Not long after, I overheard them one morning talking in bed. Their social exclusion stung, but they were still side by side, their hands touching beneath the covers, and how many people could say that? The divorces they'd seen, the betrayals and cruelties—those battles that would never be theirs. As I stood outside their room listening, I understood they had each always felt themselves to be on the outside of things. Together they were in a world of their making, a glass sphere of their own, and no one else was allowed in.

(In a funny twist, the host of that particular fateful party would later become my de facto brother-in-law on my husband's side.)

In 2002, they co-wrote *Back Then: Two Lives in 1950s New York*. My copy is signed: "To the Stein/Kaplan family, with love," an inscription of such familiarly cool impersonality that it still hurts, as though they'd handed me a book meant for someone else. There is an irony to a coauthored book, told in alternating chapters by a husband and wife, especially when they're writing about their relationship. They had chosen not to call the book a memoir but offer this description instead: "Here, then, are some personal, occasionally parallel or overlapping, narratives of life in a particular time and place." They clearly had their eyes on where they'd ended up—a long marriage and two successful careers that had led them to this authorial opportunity—and if their versions of how they'd gotten there differed, these would simply have to be sacrificed to the shared story of their marriage.

My mother's chapters are forthright and unabashed—sex on the table, for Chrissake—while my father's display his characteristic squeamishness with emotion and a tendency to defuse the reader's impulse toward sympathy: "once back in New York I went into psychoanalysis, driven by career anxiety and what romantic novelists used to call a broken heart." He pins the broken heart on the romantic novelists instead of tapping his own chest and tracing the scars on his ticker, and makes a driving force in his life look like a doodle in the bathroom stall. He mentions his difficult childhood with no quickening of his pulse, and his prose remains unruffled and offers only the glare of bright reflection, a distraction from going deeper.

"Your father was afraid of nothing," my mother added that day in the car as she turned on to the steep dirt road that led to the house. "Except maybe mice. He was terrified of mice. And big dogs."

In asking her to speculate about Joe, I am asking to be let in, but for her, guesswork feels like a form of betrayal. More importantly, asking her to dig into his psyche requires her to accept that there will always be things she doesn't know about him and questions that she never got around to asking, and this feels too much like raising and burying the dead again.

What do I do with the widow now? I can see Joe smirking, turning away from me so I can catch only half of his deep pleasure at this comical moment we find ourselves in. In a note to himself I found in a red binder that contained ideas for future projects, he had written: "Could do a funny piece about widows one of these days . . . They're all protective—vulnerable—deep-down jealous of attention paid the dead—in need of drive to get on with their own lives—let the dead lie where they fall."

Six

Between the Before and the After

•

*"He remained, in many ways, a child demand-
ing attention in a nursery which was as large as
the world."*

One winter evening when I was in my forties, I was in the
front seat of the car coming back from dinner with my father
when he ran a red light in Central Square in Cambridge and
was pulled over by the police. Stuttering, he explained that he
hadn't seen the light, that it was a mistake, that he was terribly
sorry. This was his worst nightmare, being accused of something and thought of as someone he wasn't, being questioned
by men in uniform. It was painful to see him so reduced, and
while the police checked his license, I watched sweat drip off
the end of his nose as he stared ahead in an agony of terror at
this trivial trial.

His aggrieved face was washed in color from storefront
neon lights, shadowed by cars slowing to gawk, and I had the
sense that he was feeling himself alone in a vast and unpeopled
landscape. Every orphan is someone who was abandoned and

must live with the knowledge not that abandonment could happen again, but that abandonment is a steady state that forever tilts his interaction with the world. In *A High Wind in Jamaica*—a novel he said scared him witless as a child, yet one he read over and over and had me read too—a boy falls out of a window and is never spoken of again by his family. "In the morning they might easily have thought the whole thing a dream—if [his] bed had not been so puzzlingly empty . . . Neither then nor there-after was his name ever mentioned by anybody . . . you would never have guessed from them that he had ever existed." Did my father suspect that his own disappearance, if and when it happened, wouldn't be missed?

The non-orphan grows up buffeted from the prospect of his own end by the fact that if all goes as planned, his parents will die first, but even the youngest orphan knows that he will always be next. What the rest of us fear in the most abstract way, the orphan feels in his body and the sweat that drips off his nose. And that night when my father was stopped for running a red light, he feared that some even greater crime of his was about to be discovered: the childhood crime of existing.

Guilt is a punishment for past deeds, real or imagined, and my father recognized in Twain a fellow lifelong guilt seeker, who in "reciting the past over and over again, still never found out why he was accusing himself or how he could earn forgiveness." Guilt for surviving, for thriving, was ever-present for my father too, not as a sharp pain, but as a constant ache that was best kept to himself because it couldn't ever be assuaged or dispelled.

A full moon hung above Central Square, but he wouldn't

look at it or the group of drunk college students tumbling out of the Chinese restaurant that would have made him laugh. He wouldn't take his hands from the steering wheel. He was cast out, unable to see anything on the horizon, lost, and still asking into the silence, *what is to become of me?*

I had been born knowing that my father was an orphan; for the child, that's all she needs to know. Sitting next to his silence as we awaited the cop's verdict that night, I was that girl again who had determined she wouldn't be the one to ask him questions, pull at his sorrow and drag it out into the light, who instead of adding to his burden would lessen it by taking on some of his unspoken heartache for him.

In defining his approach to Twain, he had written that how a man found his way "whether in reaction, compensation, self-protection, whether willfully or inexplicably—is one of the mysteries the biographer must at least describe if not hope to 'solve.'" As I read further into his book, I'm no longer the girl afraid of what I'll discover about both of us when I ask the questions about how he made his way, *how it felt to be him*, and where this search might finally deliver and unburden both of us.

After his parents died, Joe lived in the family apartment on New York's Upper West Side with his brother, Howard, who would eventually become his legal guardian, his maternal aunt Frances, and Georgia Edwards, a woman from Saint Kitts who had worked for the family since 1925 when my father was born. Little on the surface seemed to have changed, while below the surface, the change had to be bottomless and ever-shifting. The household still kept to the strictest dictates of observant Jewish life overseen by his aunt. My father had been dutifully observant as a child when his parents were alive, but Orthodox Judaism, he believed, had no "place for joy, spontaneity, celebration, youth; its windows were nailed shut." Sabbath services he'd attended with his brother and father had made him want to scream, and at home afterward, he had found ways to desecrate the Sabbath in his bedroom by lighting matches, fooling around with his coin collection, already as a child pushing at the boundaries of conformity, adherence, and the particular oppression of mourning.

Many decades later, having given me and my sisters no religious upbringing and the loosest affiliation to our own Jewish identity, he seemed less troubled by the contradictions that being Jewish had left him with. He wrote in *Back Then*, "My pride in belonging to a stubborn, perdurable people had come slowly, along with the recognition that, like the color of my eyes, this was for life, a membership nonelective and nonresignable, and that one better make the best of it."

But by the time he had finished his private school education where he learned about Egypt, read poetry, and shied away from organized sports, and then went to Harvard at fifteen in 1940, he was lusting after bacon, hot dogs, WASPy girls, and a new start.

By his own admission, he avoided ever thinking about his dead parents. I heard him tell people with a mixture of resignation and deflecting humor that he didn't have any idea where his parents were buried and that when he'd gone to apply for his first passport, he couldn't even remember his mother's maiden name. In notes to himself he had written, "Older than one's parents, as I am, but still one remains fixed in relation to them . . . Chaos come again. Contra-reality. Time travel." He had said in an interview, "It's been so long since I had parents that I tend to think I never had any." The claim, true or not, is heartbreaking.

His well-worn obfuscations were meant to charm, disarm, and end the line of inquiry. His past was his alone to do with what he wanted.

I had written in "The Biographer," "He knew the word on him was . . . the biographer is driven to understand the lives of others because his own history is too painful to revisit; personal details are sketchy by design. Total bullshit—no one needed to know anything about his past, they only wanted to know, felt they deserved to know."

His silence about his parents was so profound that when Michael and I named our first child Tobias, I was astounded to find out from my mother that my father's father's name had been Tobias. "Dear Georgia," he'd written after my son's birth to the woman who had raised him after his parents' deaths. "Tobias Samuel Stein, born March 31—9 pounds, 8 ounces. Beautiful child!!"

The double exclamation was an unusual frivolity: my father's scrupulous writing standards had uncharacteristically been eclipsed by sentiment. But more telling is the lack of acknowledgment of the reappearance of his father's name. If the old Tobias/new Tobias confluence touched, upset, or awed him, he never said anything to me. He never said anything about how the name sounded when it came out of my mouth, or when he used it himself.

Of the very little I knew about his father, most of it had to do with the man's passion for books, and most of it I gleaned from my father's notes. Tobias was what my father called a "serious" reader: Dostoevsky, Tolstoy, Samuel Johnson, and George Eliot. He subscribed to the Book-of-the-Month Club. He had studied to be a rabbi in Vilna before escaping to the United States in order to avoid conscription into the Russian army and had partially learned English by reading *The Last of the Mohicans*. As a widower left with two young boys, Tobias was a devoted father, rarely socialized, never remarried, and went to synagogue daily.

Twain's father, John Marshall Clemens, who died when Twain was eleven, "had been a man of precise and grammatical manners." My father described his own father in an equally cool way as "strong, contemplative, independent, and shrewd," a man who had found financial success and security, while no great passion, in creating the Dexter Shirt Company. Tobias had higher aspirations for his two sons and his eye was always on providing for their future, as though he already knew he would die from cancer six years after his wife. He filled the Upper West Side apartment with books. On his seventh birthday, my father was given *Aesop for Children*. At twelve, he received a copy of *Bartlett's Familiar Quotations*, a book that would play an important role in his life when he became its general editor for the sixteenth edition, a "job of a lifetime," fifty years later. (Pregnant with my first child, I was hired by my father to check the accuracy of thousands of quotes in the book and spent months in the Brown University library. Some days, I'd call him to share something funny I'd discovered by accident, lesser quotes lurking in the shadows of well-known ones. We forget, he said, that most people talk gobbledygook most of the time; we're lucky if we can manage to say one smart thing in a whole lifetime.)

My father wrote in *Back Then* that, "Shortly before [my father] died in February 1939 having outlived my mother by six years, he was planning to retire from the shirt business and spend the rest of his life growing Washington State apples and reading."

Here is my father's effervescent writing for me to learn from, the unruffled delivery of the devastating fact—both parents dead!—with the lighthearted specificity and punch of his father's favorite kind of apple. He could write it, beautifully and sparingly, but he couldn't speak it. There is a certain dispassion at play on the surface of things, as in much of his sections of the book, but in naming this apple, he must have also shut his eyes and conjured this particular idyll, his father still alive reaching up to pick a ripe red orb off the tree, the sun blinking behind the leaves, a pile of books, spines still unbroken, waiting for him.

I found a photograph of a woman in my father's files. I suspect she is my father's mother, but who can I ask now? I see him and myself and my youngest son in this woman whose name my father wouldn't utter. I recognize that distant, cautious look of hers in the three of us leaning back slightly when the camera points at us. She's patient and a bit long-suffering; things should be done just so and she takes her role as a Jewish wife and mother very seriously. I know little more about her beyond her passion for opera, lilacs, and her exactitude in following the observances of Jewish domestic life. She is fully lost to me, though in this photo I unearthed and was never able to ask my father about, I know something she likely doesn't know: her end is coming soon. To know her future when she doesn't binds me to her and today it is as if I have my arms around her as she absorbs the news. I would like to know what she uttered in her last minute to her sons. I would like to know what my father thought he heard her say to him, what he might have wanted her to say.

As I read the little my father writes about Twain's mother, Jane Clemens, I detect a flagging of his heart, a sag in energy. He doesn't want to do it. He doesn't have a lot to say (or too much to say that he's unable to), and the few mentions of her widowhood, her poverty, her angular and uncultivated demeanor feel desultory and chilly. As he steps into this realm of mother and son, he finds himself parched while also in deep water. In a 1966 *New York Review of Books* review of my father's biography, a reviewer noted that "the disastrous influence of his mother Jane Clemens in laying the deadly hand of convention and conformity on her son, of which [another biographer] makes so much, is not treated at all."

But when Joe wrote about Mary Mason Fairbanks, a woman Twain met aboard the *Quaker City* in 1867 during a monthslong voyage to Europe and the Holy Land that would result in his writing *The Innocents Abroad*, his noting of the parent-child dynamic in their relationship (even as Twain's mother was still alive) is robust. Twain, with his considerable rough edges and colorful past, had invited Fairbanks to work her civilizing influence on him through "maternal suasion." "For thirty-two subsequent years, Clemens addressed her as 'Mother' and called himself her 'Cub' and her 'Reformed Prodigal,' and it was in the role of son to mother that he described her to his family as 'the most refined, intelligent, and cultivated lady, and altogether the kindest and the best.'" It's a rare case in the book of my father avoiding even the briefest of psychological speculations about Twain and Fairbanks— or maybe an instance where his own unease urged him to move on quickly if he knew what was good for him.

Twain wrote that Fairbanks "sewed my buttons on, kept my clothes in presentable trim, fed me on Egyptian jam (when I behaved), lectured me awfully on the quarter deck on moonlit promenading evenings, and cured me of several bad habits." She is the idealized mother, and he smirks like a little boy when a dollop of jam lands on his shirt, when he swears or rips the knees of his pants.

But where have I seen something about buttons and mothers before?

In some 2009 notes, almost fifty years after he wrote about Twain and Fairbanks, my father wrote that Georgia had "put shirts on over my head. 'If you pop that button I won't sew it back on'—of course she sewed it." (Like Twain who said after his letters had been read without his permission, "I don't like to have those privacies exposed in such a way even to my biographer," my father would dislike my poking around his notes, but then again, he always knew I was a snoop.) And speaking of buttons, Twain had said, "Biographies are but the clothes and buttons of the man. The biography of the man himself cannot be written." My father had also written about Twain's celebrated temper triggered to tantrum by a missing button, causing him to scream and throw his shirts out of the bathroom window.

I see my father, a pale six-year-old with a dead mother and a terrible case of eczema, lifting his arms over his head so that Georgia, the woman who cared for him as if he were her own child, could dress him. Out of two lives, his and hers, he returned to the buttons between them, tiny objects of vast implication.

One afternoon when I was seventeen, my father was in a rush to go out to give a talk and he needed my help; a button had come off his shirt. With his thick, clumsy fingers, he couldn't have threaded a needle in a million years. What did he make of how careful I was not to get a needle prick of blood on the white cotton as I sat on the edge of the bed sewing on the button? Out of all the material of his life, I'm holding on to this tiny object today, a germ of how our stories grow to bigger things—and still return a single seed.

I had been putting off for too long opening a file on my father's computer desktop titled "Georgia." I already knew it would be his most private and profound material and my trespass would be tough—for both of us—because she is at the heart of his unspoken story. But the file was entirely empty, the folder an icon of intent only but still radiating unbreachable pain. How terrible for him not to have worked up the courage to tell the story of the woman who had been, in every way, his mother. He had spent more time with her than he ever had with his own mother (who, after all, had no folder with her name on it waiting to be filled. Neither did his aunt Frances, a woman I know almost nothing about). He had written how Twain nearing the end of his life and "living in mourning and seclusion . . . went underground and turned inward to the enigmas of his own life." My father, nearing the end of his life, must have sat before the blank page blemished by the computer screen's smudges and fingerprints, all jumpy desire to write about Georgia and the enigmas of his own life. There was nothing else left to write about that mattered as much as the woman who had saved him, who had kept him from going under, a woman he loved deeply. The page and I begged him to resurrect her, and himself with her in the process, but he was unable to do it.

At seventeen, Georgia Edwards had come from Saint Kitts to work for my father's family and had stayed to care for the two orphaned boys. In private notes, my father wrote that as a child he had accompanied her "while ironing & cooking in kitchen, shopping along Columbus Ave. Once in a while went to open-air markets along upper Park Avenue—wd. buy me ice cream or baked sweet potato in orange wrapping tissue. I enjoyed my sick days at home—kept G. company, watched her cook. I was pampered . . . Loyalty after my father died."

He had first introduced Georgia to my mother when they were dating as "the woman who raised me," "my real mother." Many years later in a letter he wrote to Georgia in 1988, he said, "We learned last week that Hester is going to have a baby. It's due next March. That will make four great grandchildren for you." She was my grandmother in his eyes, and I was her granddaughter, but I wasn't aware of this. She loomed mythically large, her name spoken with reverence by him, but I barely knew her and had seen her only a handful of times in my life. In her last decades, she lived in Co-Op City in the Bronx in an apartment my uncle Howard had bought her. I could see the cluster of buildings from the highway on the way into Manhattan. She was that close, just on the other side of the car window, but we didn't stop. My father wrote to her and talked to her on the phone regularly, and he visited her and sat in her living room where she kept his books and a folder of his letters and newspaper clippings about him on a side table. But my sisters and I never visited, not even when I lived in New York.

I had always known that Georgia had left her own two boys at home with her husband, Willie, in order to raise my father and his brother. In "The Biographer," I described the biographer's feelings: "When he'd thought about her boys who were his and his brother's ages, he'd assumed they hated him, and he didn't blame them. He couldn't find any fairness in the way their lives and his intersected, how they'd lost what he'd won, and how he loved their mother deeply, wordlessly, and with great shame." The problem was, as I found out in a letter to her from him, I was entirely wrong about this; Georgia had no children. From the earliest age, I had invented those boys as a way to lessen the injustice I'd always felt about the situation, to give her something of her own, to relieve and protect my father from his own guilt.

"Dear Georgia," he wrote her in 1937 when he was twelve and she was just about thirty. "I hope that you are well and that you will soon be out of the hospital and back here. The new maid is alright but she is not half as good as you are . . . Another thing I don't like is that if she serves something I like one night I will have it every night until I'm just plain sick of it. The only thing that makes somebody like a thing is that they don't get it everyday. She doesn't seem to realize that . . . I have nothing else to say so I will close my letter wishing you Love and Health. Joseph. P.S. You may be interested to know that some of the boys in my class and their mothers asked about you."

Georgia had been in the hospital for a hysterectomy, my mother confirmed, but my father wouldn't have known this then, or how for a young Black woman in 1937, this was most likely the only treatment offered her. He did not have access to her experience as a Black employee of a white family, but he'd witnessed his own parents behave toward her in ways that made him "shrivel with shame." While his desktop folder on Georgia was empty, he had typed some notes about her and put them in a notebook, but so filled with dishonor he had been unable to write about her in full sentences. "Awful seeing [Georgia] have to wear formal maid's uniform—black with white collar and apron. One occasion was my mother's Hadassah tea party. All such uniforms came from dept. store 'Domestics.'" Georgia and Willie were made to eat in the kitchen at Howard's wedding in the mid-1950s. "Should have made a fuss, or moved to the kitchen. Still ashamed of myself for inaction," he wrote.

Georgia's decision to stay on and raise my father and his brother—to "take charge," as he described it—acquires poignant significance when my father's notes on his relationship with her don't take up what her life beyond him was like. Perhaps he didn't know or failed to consider, or his perception and memory of her were too bound by the desperate exigencies of that period in his own life. Fragments display his first forays into exploring the troubling reality and facing his role in it: "Major problem here: the egoism of the growing boy. Took for granted stereotype of the faithful black mother substitute (but a servant nonetheless). 'Everybody' had a black maid, most of the time a live-in. Horrible little rooms. Segregation."

When I visited home from New York during college, my father sometimes asked me to stop by one of the kosher butchers on Broadway and buy calves' feet for ptchah, a dish he had learned to make from Georgia who had learned it from his mother and grandmother. He recalled in his notes Georgia at the butcher shop, jostling in a crowd of Jewish women, their cooks and housemaids, telling the butcher that she wanted the calves' feet sawed instead of cleavered. I was to insist on that, too. On the packed Greyhound bus to Boston, I was the only one carrying bloody bones nestled in ice. The smell of them boiling away for hours on the stove was foul and permeated everything. The look of the dish—"a stiff jelly of a yellowish cast, that held in suspension bits of gristle, carrot, onion and garlic"—was bad and the taste even worse. But when my father, standing at the counter and slurping up spoonfuls of the stuff, shut his eyes and pronounced it glorious, he was returned to the kitchen as a boy, close to Georgia's side by the stove. She had taught him how to cook, and his solitary and ambitious projects—sauerkraut, ginger beer, stews—filled the house with what I now understand were the smells of his past, his missing her and finding solace as he leaned against her hip.

Georgia and Willie attended Susanna's wedding at our house. My father in a buoyant mood had arranged pots of flowers on the deck and cleaned up the backyard. He looked transported holding Georgia's frail arm as he walked her across the uneven grass to her seat at the front. I was mesmerized by this unguarded display that I'd never seen him make with anyone else. But he didn't share Georgia with me, not really, so that he might say to me and to her, see, I survived, I grew, I thrived, and here is the woman who saved me and here is my boundless gratitude, here is my past brought into my present. He didn't tell me when Georgia died and he went alone to her funeral, as though his grief, if he shared it, would turn wild and devour everything.

After Willie died, he wrote a letter to Georgia, breathtaking in its full and open feelings for her: "Do you remember when you came to visit us on Cape Cod, that you and I walked down the road and you pointed out to me a little cedar tree? It's the only cedar tree in that whole stretch, but I never noticed it until you came. Anyhow, ever since then I've taken special care of that tree, pruned the growth around it to let in more light and air. The cedar is much bigger and stronger and greener now than when you saw it. It's our Georgia tree."

Sometimes my father walked down the road in Truro with

his giant pruning shears or his machete, which he liked to sharpen and swing through the tall grass and low-hung locust branches. On most days, his mission was maintenance, and maybe some clearing of his head. If on certain days he only tended to the Georgia tree, which I never knew about, it was done in private.

Recently, I searched for the tree, but couldn't find it. Anything could have happened to it after thirty years in an unforgiving climate, and it was impossible to know where even to begin in the overgrowth, but to write about it keeps it alive.

Seven

Making His Way

•

*"In order to recapture his past he must follow
a familiar pattern of rebirth and becomes less
rather than more like his old self."*

One summer afternoon, I was a mopey teenager draped over
the back of the sagging couch in the living room. The dog
was stretched out on the floor in front of me. A bowl of soft-
ening pretzels left over from a party a week earlier was on
the coffee table, and it might be a few more days before the
many dirty glasses, some still with darkening booze, were
cleared away. One of the guests at that party had forgotten a
blue sweater with pearl buttons; it would stay on the back of
a chair for years, my parents speculating as to why its owner
never came back for it. The house had a sharply sour smell as
humidity seeped into old rugs, the spines of a million books,
the widening cracks of the horsehair plaster walls, the narrow
back stairway.

Just across the hall from me and beyond the coat and
boot–choked foyer (winter things were never put away but

just waited until their season rolled around again), my father was writing in his study. Through the closed door, I heard the words marching out in unbroken lines from his typewriter. It was a mystery to me how he could write without hesitation and with almost metronomic certainty when spoken attempts to express himself were halting and evasive, but already I knew he was a different man when he was at work. *Mr. Clemens and Mark Twain* had been published seven years earlier, and my father was now The Biographer. People wanted to interview him, ask for his advice, connections, and favors. He was invited to give talks and lectures, publish essays and forewords and book reviews. He had a publisher who took him out to fancy, boozy lunches at the Four Seasons in New York, and for Christmas—which we, full Jews, half celebrated—bound his books in leather with gold-stamped lettering on the spine. He had New York's top literary agent who sometimes called just before dinnertime. *Christ, hang up the fucking phone*, my father would yell from his study, where he'd run with his gin and tonic to pick up the extension so he could talk in private.

The typing stopped and my father came out of his study in saggy shorts and a ratty T-shirt. He shut the door behind him and tested it to make sure it was closed. He didn't see me only feet away as he sailed somewhere on the sea of his work, and whether that sea was smooth or choppy, I couldn't tell yet, but I knew he was still writing in his head as his bare feet shushed across the floor and he absently scratched his forearms. He had written that Twain "never pawed, he was no back-slapper or arm-squeezer, he avoided touching other people. He was excitable, easily hurt, desperately hungry for affection and tenderness, often depressed, capable of great rage and greater remorse," and that day, attuned to his movements and his shades, I felt a familiar anxious uncertainty about what mood he might be in. His warmth was unpredictable and often hard to detect, like feeling the morning sun's heat locked in an evening stone.

When the dog got up to meet him, my father noticed me on the couch. He blinked, puzzled by my existence: Who are you and how did you get in here?

"Jesus, it's hot," he said. His study was the only room in the house with an AC. "What are you doing?"

"Nothing," I said.

He cleared his throat, his tell of distress at my squandered minutes. He told me to go read a book but I told him I didn't have one, which was like saying I didn't have snow in a blizzard. Every surface in the house was covered with them. I was surrounded by them even then, art books to my left, volumes of poetry at the far end of the room, glossy new books on the table in front of me. Books were piled on and below tables and benches and beds, crowded the stair risers, hid in the closet between the sheets and towels. I knew the particular sound of a new book in a padded mailer being pushed through the mail slot. There were wild heaps of books on the floor of the sunporch as though an earthquake had shaken them off their shelves. There were books in drawers, on the backs of toilets, on the kitchen table, in the back of the car and under the seats. There were often cartons of new books in Joe's study when he was judging a literary award, each book radiating impossible hope. The cupboard at the stair landing was jammed with copies of the books my parents had written, and when I opened it, they came tumbling out, gasping for light and attention, and I shoved them back in like unwanted siblings. I once left a paperback out in the rain just to watch it swell up and die. I loved books and I also hated them, dog-earing pages, using them as coasters to torture my father. I wrote in them, used yellow highlighters (an abomination in his eyes), stood them up to prop open my bedroom windows.

"Go to the library, then," he said, wearily. "I hear they have books there."

For years I had accompanied him on his trips to Harvard's Widener Library. I was the only child ever there and I was devout and quiet as I trailed him up the marble steps. The library had been a gift to the university from a woman to memorialize her son who had died on the *Titanic*, a fact that gave the place a morbid dim. I also knew that *perished*, not *died*, was the right word in this context, as was *souls*, and not *people*. The art inside, particularly the two Sargent paintings in the main stairwell—*Death and Victory* and *Entering the War*— gave me some sense of the earthly and moral importance of what went on in that gray place. On each trip, I silently read the inscription on the landing—*Dulce et decorum est Pro patria mori*. My father wouldn't tell me what it meant because he wanted me to figure it out by myself. Try, he urged. What do those words sound like?

My father exchanged a nod if he ran into someone he knew, but there was no stopping to chat. Even the posture of the students suggested the weight of intellectual pursuit. My father wandered through the open stacks, tilting his head to read titles, pulling a book from the shelf to read a few pages while the timed lights ticked off their remaining seconds before the stacks were thrown into darkness again. The stacks, like the card catalog, my father told me, could yield great surprises if you just looked left and right of what you'd come for. It was a way to open up your thinking.

My father's standards for writing were impossibly high, but he was no snob when it came to reading and a good story. He never censored my choices, perhaps to encourage me to develop my own discernment. He'd gotten me to read *Queen Victoria* by Lytton Strachey along with the collected works of celebrity biographer Kitty Kelley, whom he later called "the Saddam Hussein of privacy invasion," and whose books he read and industry he admired. (About her biography of Nancy Reagan, he'd said, "There wasn't much left of Mrs. Reagan after Kelley finished with her, except perhaps for a mound of beak and feathers.") Also, *The Passion Flower Hotel*, about a group of girls at a fancy boarding school who run a prostitution ring, and *A Dance to the Music of Time* by Anthony Powell. I'd added *The Happy Hooker* by Xaviera Hollander, R. Crumb, Charles Dickens, and Judith Krantz (who made up part of my steady diet of novels about sex and money and how far a woman could get in the world if she had good breasts). Unlike Twain, my father had no illusions that "American girls did not read smutty novels . . . and were unacquainted with 'unclean thoughts.'"

Recently, I had stopped going to Widener with him and had started going alone to the Cambridge Public Library.

Armed with a library card and the key to my bike lock, I was sure I was taking the necessary steps to becoming a serious person, someone who might one day sit at the kitchen table and give her opinion about a book. I was on a heady quest as I went into the stacks, armed with a call number I'd written on scrap paper, even as the quest remained entirely undefined. I wasn't ever fooled by my own pretense, though, and found that what I really liked most about being alone in the stacks of that old library was the floor of cloudy glass bricks that allowed me to see people moving above and below me, as though I were suspended in a place that wasn't here or there.

But a week earlier in those stacks, I had become convinced that a man was following me, ducking and disappearing around corners. I heard his shallow breathing, even smelled his funk. When I hurried to a different floor just to be sure, his footsteps followed mine in the stairwell. I told myself not to be prissy—a terrible thing to be if you were the middle of two tough sisters—and that it was probably nothing. Nothing unless he wanted to rape or kill me. The world was full of menace: parents who died; the Boston Strangler, who I was sure had prowled our street and would one night enter through my bedroom window; Kitty Genovese, who'd uselessly screamed for help before she was murdered; the man who'd exposed himself to me in front of William James Hall, Harvard's psychology building, as if he were begging to be swept inside and cured.

I ran out of the stacks, past the desk where a librarian sat, and out of the building. I couldn't fit the key into the bike lock because my hands were shaking. Back in my room at home, I tried to soothe myself by saying I'd only imagined I was being followed. Nothing terrible had happened, so that proved I was in fact being prissy. It didn't occur to me to have told the librarian—or anyone else about something that, in the end, didn't happen.

I wanted to tell my father about that day but I was afraid he wouldn't know how to comfort me, which would have been worse than not being comforted at all. The idea that my mother would soon also hear because he would tell her would leave me having to manage her reaction, and that seemed almost worse. But what really stopped me was this: What was my fear compared to my father's at my age? Trivial, meaningless, not worth mentioning. Fear is compounded by the knowledge that there is no one to rescue you from it, and terror never exposed to the light becomes an abyss.

But when I said I didn't want to go to the library, he looked at me curiously and told me to hold on. He went into his study and returned with a copy of *The Count of Monte Cristo*.

"Read this," he said. I see now that he sensed my melancholy and offered the book as a cure—a cure he couldn't provide himself—and a way to see ahead.

In 2003, at the age of seventy-eight, my father published an essay in *The American Scholar* titled "Treasure and Vengeance." In it he wrote that "even the happiest children occasionally enjoy fantasies about some terrible injustice they imagine they've suffered and they sob themselves to sleep. Motherless from the age of seven [in other instances, he claims he was six when she died, a telling inconsistency], I was far from the happiest of children, and I became adept at creating delectable fantasies of a familiar sort." He acknowledged his past and diminished the significance of it at the same time, one of his best sleights of hand. He wanted everyone to believe that he was no different from other children.

His particular fantasies involved his widowed father, Tobias, remarrying "the mother of all wicked stepmothers" who treated him like a dog before committing him to a snowy orphanage. "No resolution, no forgiveness on my part or contrition on theirs. But what a banquet of rage, misery, and self-pity I had fed on! I had been playwright, director, and actor in my own theater."

My father credits *The Count of Monte Cristo*, which he'd pulled from the shelves of the New York Public Library as a kid, with providing some of the kindling for these particular fantasies, but I didn't know this when he gave me the book to read that day. He didn't say anything about its significance for him when I found him making iced tea in the kitchen a week later and I got up the courage to tell him how thrilling it was when Edmond Dantès sews himself into another man's shroud and gets tossed into the sea, the cemetery of Château d'If.

"It's terrific stuff," he said, mildly, and ready to go back to work.

"At the age of thirty-three," my father had written in that essay, "... Dantès reenters ... as the Count of Monte Cristo, a suave and mysterious man of seemingly limitless wealth and many identities." Accused of a crime he did not commit (as the orphan accuses himself of the crime of his parents' demise and tosses in everything else for good measure), the man is reborn, rich, free, shrugging off the burden of his history, exacting vengeance as he sees fit.

As a child reading the book, my father could not have given voice to the emotional reverberations he felt. But in rereading it many years later, he discovered a new adult resonance for himself in the pages. "Dumas is careful to point out that when Edmond Dantès makes his escape, he is thirty-three years old, a canonical age for starting over," he wrote. "I cherish a particularly warm feeling about the matter of Edmond's age: it was at thirty-three that I left a publishing career in New York to write my first book." (I was about the same age when I finally wrote my first full story.) This notion that transformation and the creation of a new identity are possible at this age is central to how my father saw his own—and Twain's—biography. That he saw his own life's arc reflected in a novel suggests his belief in the truths of fiction, and the reader's (and the writer's) ability to imagine a more daring and fully realized life.

"In reality, every reader is, while he is reading, the reader of his own self," Proust (his favorite writer) wrote, so is it possible that I've had this backward all this time? Maybe Joe wasn't only showing me something about himself when he gave me that book, but showing me how I might discover something about myself and all I might imagine about my future.

When he was eighty-two, my father began to write about his last season at Schroon Lake Camp in the red binder of notes.

When I'd found several issues of the *Schroon Lake Camp Chronicle* high up on a shelf in the Cambridge apartment, it struck me that because his decline with Parkinson's was slow and inevitable, he had time to decide what he would leave to be found—not by his wife, who would no longer look, but by his children. Each day he spent stuffing his papers, letters, and notes down the trash chute and holding on to others, he was shaping the biography of himself for me.

"Summer of 1941, my third year there," he wrote. "I was 15 and going to Harvard in Sept. So I did whatever I wanted: mainly read Byron . . . [and played baseball] Occasionally someone would hit fly to r.f. The ball seemed to hang in the air but bound for catastrophe; my body tensed. The ball would either go over my head or hit me in the chest. Predictable humiliation. After a while I refused to play baseball. A summer of liberating lawlessness and solo behavior opposite to what camp experience—discipline & group behavior—is supposed to be, sneaked into town at night, smoked, drank beer went hunting with my rifle before reveille—dug up old grave (part way)—shot rats at garbage dump—lucky hip-shot at pheasant—shot up old Ford—removed its magneto—wired it to my iron cot frame: shock treatment for counselors! Paddles as punishment—thrown into lake at night."

Camper Joseph, as he is called in his profile in the *Chronicle*, looks and sounds like an all-around affable kid, integrated and popular, with a well-built self-possession that the other boys lack. In a group portrait, his posture is too straight for a kid his age, but he's his own keeper and reminds himself not to invite curiosity, attention, or pity by rounding his shoulders or being sullen. He can't conceive that others may have suffered as he has. To him they appear untouched by misfortune while he is wrapped in it.

But his tone describing that last summer before college, an orphan for a couple of years already, full of the boy's bravura and carnal thrill at his transgressive and solo behavior, belies his rage behind the gleeful shooting of rats and the deconsecration of the grave. In his half-hearted attempt to empty and explore its contents, to uncover the dead and see the whole person reanimated, he presaged his life as a biographer.

When I was twelve, I'd discovered a hidden closet in my grandparents' basement. I was not a brave kid or a rule-breaker, but my impulse had been unstoppable, and I pushed aside the file cabinet that hid the door, took out the taped-up box inside, cut through it to find a can containing the ashes of my grandfather's mother. It was a discovery so vastly beyond what I had imagined I might find, that even today its implications are barely graspable. Later that day, I confessed to my father what I'd done, but there was no punishment, and nothing more said. Decades later, I heard him ask in a lecture on the culture of biography, "Is a biographer a grave robber, or a body snatcher?" Today, I like to think he had both of us in mind.

The assertion of my father's freedom to do as he pleased that last summer at camp—*Look! There is no one to stop me!*— is the same assertion of his aloneness—*Look! There is no one to stop me!* When he was finally caught for his mischief by the counselors, he wrote, "they were surprised it was me. Always the innocent." My father recognized the usefulness and power in this particular familiar masquerade, when he wrote that for Twain it was "a stance [he] constantly polished: the genteel naïf, the bookish dupe."

When I put the years' camp group portraits side by side, I am practicing my father's art of storytelling by creating a narrative that's driven by the needs and conflicts of the character, my father. I first see the skinny boy who one summer desperately imagines his mother emerging from between the pines to take him home. She has been dead now longer than he knew her alive. He's grinning enough to show that he's heard the photographer's command but already understands that there is no connection between his face and his feelings.

Several summers later, with his father gone too, his chest hardened and his muscles thickened, I see that he has perfected the bland smile and the art of disguise; it comes naturally to him at this point. He understands no one is coming for him, doesn't even imagine it anymore. He has become the divided self with the divided heart out of a will to prevail, but he is no more loyal to one self than to the other, no self more real than the other. The boy in the picture with the best posture is the one who hides the heaviest sadness, and he enters college that fall, determined to keep his trauma and confusions to himself and bear what he called "the stigmas of alleged niceness and normality in a resigned way." No one will really know him, but that's the choice he's made.

Soon after I found my father's camp notes, I called his friend Steve, whom he had met at camp, and told him I was writing this book. By way of introduction, Steve told me, my father had explained that he lived in the care of his older brother Howard, his aunt, and the family's housekeeper.

"Joe was a very private person," Steve added, amused by the obvious understatement. He said that in the following eight decades of their very close friendship, my father never mentioned his parents or his situation. Not once. "And I felt I shouldn't ask," he said. "Let me know what you learn. He was very proud of your writing, by the way."

Something clicked into place, part sorrow for what I'd never heard from my father, part new certainty that he was with me writing this book. I pictured Steve on his patio overlooking Long Island Sound where I had visited a few times, the last time for his wife's funeral, both of us considering my father and everything he'd kept to himself. When Steve died of COVID early in the pandemic and only months after our conversation, I felt as if the earth had suddenly swallowed all the old men up.

As a girl, I compulsively rearranged my bedroom, sometimes several times a month, dragging all the furniture across the floor. One afternoon, Joe walked by my open door and stopped to help me move my bed by the window. When he asked why I was doing it, he seemed genuinely interested about all those times he'd heard the scraping and banging just above his head. When I told him I liked waking in the middle of the night and feeling I was somewhere and someone unfamiliar, of dragging myself out of sleep into my real life and then back into dream again, he nodded as though he too knew this sensation of being lost and found, of being not himself.

I want to tell him today that three years after he gave me *The Count of Monte Cristo*, I was assaulted in a cheap hotel while on a trip with some high school friends. I had gone back to the room before the others because I wasn't feeling well and called the front desk to say that none of the lights were working. I was told someone would be right up, and when that someone came into the room, he insisted that I needed to face the light fixture on the wall and hold it steady for him while he stood behind me. I froze as I watched his charade of unscrewing the dusty light bulb, fiddling with the socket, tapping something with his useless screwdriver while he pressed himself into me, breathed into my neck, thrust his hips into me, and groped me. I never told my father or anyone else about it, not even my friends when they returned. I took the experience into every relationship with men, but I'd learned from my father to keep these trials hidden and mine them for their heat in writing instead.

For years, I've carried around a stained essay by Padgett Powell called "Learning to Hit Back," as if I knew I'd always arrive at this moment of admission, even if it took me years: "I do not feel so hot today because I suspect that we are yet being told by brutes to sit against the wall while the nonmeek inherit the earth . . . One gets the large feeling of returning home most days without hitting back. That little nausea is at the root, perhaps, of deciding to write—deciding at last, however feebly, to defend oneself, to hit back."

Dantès's emergence from the burlap sack, blue with cold,

gasping for breath, and clinging to a rock in the harbor, sounds just like birth, and today I also want to tell my father that everything I knew about life was brought to bear on Dantès's survival and mine in that shitty hotel room.

"The farther [Twain] got from home the more attractive the fields and cities of the republic seemed," my father wrote, suggesting that by harnessing the past's power, one could go forward instead of back, and embrace the fullest measure of life. This notion has the urgency and muscle of persistence, as propulsive a force for him as it was for Edmond Dantès bursting from his watery shroud into the sharp air of new purpose, as propulsive as it is for me today.

Eight

Poised

•

"[Twain] still had no sure sense of identity or vocation. It was only by a wayward and dilatory process that Mark Twain, who had probably the most richly endowed natural talent in American literature, finally gave himself over to writing the book that established his fame."

Like Twain, who said he learned to write by "setting up acres of good and bad literature" in the printing office and distinguishing between the two, my father in his twenties began his own of process of learning to write by taking a series of temporary editing and writing jobs, including a textbook about psychosomatic diagnosis (a poignant choice for a man with a chronic skin condition exacerbated by stress), a dictionary, a Bible, and editions of Thoreau, Shakespeare, Walt Whitman, Plato, and Aristotle. But even as he excelled at it, there was no fire in him for this kind of work. In my late twenties, after holding jobs in book and magazine publishing, I worked, mostly unhappily, as a ghostwriter—on books about skin cancer, children of alcoholics, dermatologists in the Nazi era, how to wash your face properly. I wrote something called a business novel for a successful CEO who believed that fictionalizing an abstract concept would produce a useful teaching tool. It didn't, but only in part because he insisted that all the good and trustworthy women in the novel be long-legged and blond, and all the underhanded and conniving ones be thick-waisted, short, and dark.

Ghostwriting was top-notch schooling in how to craft a sentence, an idea, and an argument—very often out of pure nonsense and arrogance. But the work was also a daily exercise in sublimation, and while I was good at it, I suffered from the same ambivalence my father had about laboring with material that didn't belong to me and I couldn't believe in. My uneasiness with such writing was further compounded by my father's obvious but unspoken disappointment in how I was spending my time. At least, I consoled myself, he thought I had better things to do with my brain. I had a distant notion of wanting to write my own stories, even if I had no idea how, despite all my reading and listening and watching people who did, but I was far from confessing this to myself at the time. (I had written only one very short story years before when I was ten. In the second paragraph, everyone in the bucolic seaside town gets swept away by a tsunami.) I did recognize though that to go into the family business was to ask for big trouble. The children of writers I knew who became writers themselves suffered from all the obvious pitfalls: unavoidable competition and comparison, the often unwitting rehashing of family dynamics every time they sat down to write, and their sense—and others'—that their success, if there was any to be had, was only because of who their parents were. I was so determined to avoid these snares that only one time, out of desperation, did I ask my enormously connected father, who very often helped other writers he barely knew, for help finding an agent. While he reluctantly agreed to send the manuscript to his, I knew I'd breached some unspoken family rule. He couldn't say no, but I had put him in an awkward position that made him un-happy. I'm not certain if he read the novel before he sent it off, but nothing was ever said about it again. I never heard back from his agent, though I suspected my father had re-ceived but couldn't get himself to deliver the bad news to me, and I couldn't ever bring myself to ask. Almost fifteen years later, I finally heard from an assistant in that agent's office: they were moving, had found my manuscript in a box on a shelf, and they wanted to know if they should send it back to me or just throw it out.

"Another stage of mystification has begun," my father as a young man had written to a girlfriend. He'd kept these letters in a file cabinet, perhaps to remind himself—and me—just how lost he'd been. "I'm not sure of my shape." He called himself a jellyfish. "I am not really interested in the insides of publishing, although some conscience—my father's ghost—tells me that I ought to be and often has me wholly convinced that I am. I think I may be approaching a point of honesty about what I really want to do; and it involves some pain and some fright . . . in personal terms it means going out on a limb (which I usually avoid doing)."

Not ready to face the pain and fright yet of this particular inkling and limb-climbing—he didn't dare say the word *write* any more than I did—his father's ghost won out and he stayed in publishing, eventually becoming an editor at Simon & Schuster. But after a few years of "meetings, alcoholic agents, and infantilized authors who assumed editors were writing teachers," Joe, married by then, dared to begin admitting to himself that a career in publishing, even a potentially brilliant one, wasn't ever going to be for him. Despite the promise his mentors, including Max Schuster, saw in their protégé, this fatherless son with a searing intelligence knew there was something missing, and that there were more exciting things to be done: his own writing.

"The truth . . . was not that I hated my job. I hated myself for not loving it more and doing it better and for spending too much time looking out the window at the crowds." he wrote in *Back Then*. His walks along the Hudson River when he should have been at his desk working on a manuscript or having lunch with an author returned him to the familiar ground of his own company and those stirrings to write. That sensual and visceral urge, that subterranean draw that involves the skin, the heart, and the blood—the urge I would finally give in to myself—describes my father's deepest longing to create something of his own. Not simply something to be read and considered, but something to be held, the physicality of the bound object, the evidence of its author's existence.

In his seventies, he had written in some notes, "I still

fantasize about showing things to my parents, especially my father, but now feel they are not only invisible but ultimately permissive, leaving me free to become what I am . . . what I've done, the different kind of life I've lived from anything they might have imagined." His sentences are intimate and full of desire for the impossible to be made possible, and the longing that might finally allow him to write about what mattered most, what he had yet to wrangle. He had pictured his parents, had they lived, turning a page of a book he'd written with a proud finger gliding across the top to the righthand corner, then that elegant cornering descent, as I had been taught by him to do. The hands that hold the book are alive again. I would like to give him this book I'm writing.

Joe knew that he would be taking a big risk leaving publishing to write a book, as vague a concept as that still was, and that it might be foolish at best, disastrous at worst. He was a new father, and maybe this was not the time to do something crazy. But the *idea* of writing a book, his own book instead of someone else's, once it had taken hold, occupied him in a way nothing else ever had. I have felt the same shiver and laugh that swirled in his chest when he decided to climb out on that delicate, dangerous limb and write.

He hadn't decided what he would write about yet or what form this writing might take, but he knew what had always interested him, and wrote in *Back Then* that he "was hopelessly in love with the American nineteenth century—it was just far enough and near enough in time to be both strange and familiar, historical and contemporary." Hopelessly and uninhibitedly in love, beyond reason, the idea is impossible to shake; it demands to be let out of its cage. "Mathew Brady's portraits—brought the dead out of their graves and gave them an eerie, compelling, staring presence, as if they had just brushed past me out of the dark and were about to whisper in my ear. What was it like to have lived their lives, to have seen the great pulsating nineteenth century through their eyes?" he asked.

For Joe, the portraits, with their subjects' eyes "fixed in the spectral stare," brought the dead out of their graves rather than capturing the subjects while they were alive because this is the biographer's lens of revivification, and he was already moving toward his form when he looked at those men. ("Perhaps," Julian Barnes wrote in *Flaubert's Parrot*, "this is the advantage of making friends with those already dead: your feelings towards them never cool.")

He had written that Twain early on had "groped" toward his material as a writer, suggesting that he knew just how clumsy and slippery the pursuit could be. Still, of those early stirrings in search of his material, my father had later written in the memoir, in a post hoc corralling of all the messy, deeply personal, and incongruous impulses that "what I needed was a subject or an event that could be brought to a dramatic focus in individual lives."

Having spent years in psychoanalysis, starting in his early twenties, my father might have been aware of Freud's claim that biographers "are fixated on their heroes in a very peculiar manner. They frequently select the hero as the object of study because, for personal reasons of their own emotional life, they had a special affection for him from the very outset." Freud had also said the biographical truth was unattainable, and that "to be a biographer you must tie yourself up in lies, concealments, hypocrisies, false colorings, and even in hiding a lack of understanding." Just outside my father's study, there was a framed photograph of my mother's great-uncle Freud and the congratulatory note he'd sent to my grandparents on the occasion of her birth. Of the thousands of times Joe passed by it, he must have stopped from time to time to tell the old man to lighten up.

One evening in the spring of 1959, my parents went to see Hal Holbrook's one-man show, *Mark Twain Tonight!* "Three hours of make-up transformed a thirty-five-year-old actor into a seventy-year-old spellbinding monologist," my awe-struck father observed. Twain had always been part of his literary landscape, but here the man was alive on the stage, sweating, pacing, his spit flying. Holbrook had brought the dead out of the grave, allowing Twain to whisper in my father's ear: pick me, pick me, pick me. Holbrook's telling that night of Twain's ghost story, "The Golden Arm," was so terrifying that my father claimed it almost put my mother into labor.

"All the 'accidents' of Mark Twain's life had some kind of purposive meaning—so it seemed to him in his old age, when he tried to map out the turning points by which he had become a writer," my father wrote, and when he talked about why he became a writer and chose Mark Twain as the subject of his first book, there's also the suggestion of accident and the aligning stars at play, unexplainable forces of affinity and attraction, of unconscious drives. My parents might just as easily have gone to the movies, or stayed in that night, and our stories would be entirely different. After all, I was there that night in the theater, too; that was me, enchanted as I listened from the womb.

When Holbrook died in 2021, my mother wrote to *The New York Times.*

Re: "Hal Holbrook, Actor Who Channeled Mark Twain, Is Dead at 95": "Mr. Holbrook's portrayal of Mark Twain was not impersonation: it was possession. My late husband, Justin Kaplan, and I went to see Mr. Holbrook's performance in 1959. Justin was so moved by what he saw and heard on that small stage in a hotel that he decided to write a biography of Twain. That book, 'Mr. Clemens and Mark Twain,' my husband's first effort, won both the National Book Award and the Pulitzer Prize in 1967. To say that Mr. Holbrook's performance was unforgettable is not doing it justice."

Soon after Holbrook's show, which Joe was still high from days later, a publishing mentor took him out to lunch and suggested that he look into Twain as a subject. Within fifteen minutes of considering it, Joe was "thunderstruck in love with the idea," and after lunch went out to buy whatever he could find of Twain's work.

"I spent the afternoon in my office reading *Roughing It*; the evening at the Harvard Club Library reading Albert Bigelow Paine's authorized biography of Mark Twain; and the next several weeks, on company time, doing the most single-minded and happiest thinking of my life," he explained in *Back Then.* "More awake than ever, more concentrated, at the same time I had the sort of warm, suffusing sensation (Keats's 'drowsy numbness') you have when you suddenly find something valuable and necessary you've been a long time looking for and never altogether expected to find, in this case it was a vocation as well as a book idea."

Modesty kept him from claiming as his own the word *drowse*, one that Twain used often enough that it is feathered with meaning when my father uses it. "'Drowsing' was [Twain's] talismanic word to evoke the landscape of dream," he wrote. "The word conjured up an image of childhood purified by the years, a state of idyllic innocence which could be recaptured only in the imagination."

Keats asks, "Was it a vision, or a waking dream?" The moment was both when Twain became the man of my father's present and future. As he sat in that paneled room, the book he had open on his lap fell to the floor and broke the quiet. Other men in the room, humorless and patrician, regarded this big-nosed kid with irritation. He imagined, as Twain had, the possibility that his own history might direct rather than stymy his future, its energy of loss and survival converted into insight. He felt the thrill of his own possible hatching as he read about Sam Clemens becoming Mark Twain.

Wildly awake and charged up, he ignored the disapproving men clearing their throats. This path toward biography now looked like the highway he'd always been preparing to navigate, studying the maps and plotting the course through all his years of uncertainty about what would become of him. When he left the club, the weather had turned wild in the dark. He smelled the concrete readying itself for rain. As he walked home, the certainty of his decision felt like slipping into a bed that had been warmed for his arrival and where he might have a dream of his past so vivid and purified that for a moment he can be a child full of all possibility, and when he writes, his parents are there to read.

It's the spring of 1964 in Joe's study, five years already invested in the book. He admires the steady progress he's making, but don't ask him how it's coming or when he thinks he'll be finished. (It will be, soon.) Every day he gets into the ring with his heavily muscled doubts and has to duke it out. Sometimes he emerges bruised, and yesterday was one of those days. His eczema had been driving him nuts, and without even a nod at restraint, he'd scratched up and down his arms and legs until he bled, and then he'd taken a long cold shower and a long walk by the Charles River with the dog, followed by two tall gin and tonics, some Brie and crackers, and my mother's attention, just to ease his agitation.

Even after all that, he'd woken at 3:00 a.m., shaking and thinking of how much was riding on this book, and asked himself once again, *What have I done?* A few days earlier, he'd taken me and Susanna to the Harvard Museum of Natural History just down the street and through the Divinity School parking lot. In the Africa Gallery, where giant stuffed animals stood stoically behind glass, the air reeking of mothballs and dust on the radiators, I had squatted to examine the underbelly of the lion. When my father crouched next to me, I had pointed out where the seams in the skin had started to split, revealing wire sutures and stuffing. For him, this was part of the imperfect, fusty pleasure of the place, but I was upset by the shattered notion that these were real animals stilled just for me when I visited. Tears fell from behind my tortoiseshell glasses, ones that looked just like his. He didn't know what to say to me, how to explain it. But as we moved on to another part of the museum and stopped at the diorama of a Nootka whaling scene, everything frozen in perfect detailed miniature, he saw my delight return. He watched me animate and enter into another life—a piece of painted glass was water, red paint was the blood of a butchered whale on the hard plaster of white snow—and knew that he was witnessing me discover the power of my own imagination. He had seen a child lose a kind of faith and gain another at the same time. He is sure this is what writing requires, and this morning, he wants to use all this life around him.

At this point, he's been at this long enough to have discovered that writing a book is not a straight line from the first page to the last; instead, it is circular, it is retreading and refining. He didn't know how or what moved Twain when he started this, much as I didn't about him when I began; the man was a shell to him then, a placeholder for time, ideas, and intentions. But he knows Twain well enough now to find his confident and easy passage from writer to subject as he returns to the very first chapter, which he feels sits inertly and a little bloodlessly on the page. He crosses out what he'd written years earlier and types instead, "Standing on the deck of the sidewheeler *America* of the Opposition Line as it left San Francisco at noonday in bright sunlight on December 15, 1866.

Sam Clemens, just turned thirty-one, was facing eastward toward his future and leaving the frontiers which nurtured him, which he celebrated and eventually symbolized."

It is no struggle for him to imagine Twain's feet firmly planted on the deck of that sidewheeler, and he feels the same rocking underneath his feet and the same sun on his face. He smells the same cold briny air. His eyelids are half-mast so he doesn't lose this sensation of inhabiting another person because he knows that describing the texture and density of someone else's experience is the way to bring an event to life.

He hears the van that delivers chicken, milk, and fruit on Wednesdays pull up in front of the house; the sound of the idling engine becomes the waves against the sidewheeler.

He knows that if you put a man on a boat bound for his life's adventure, add water and weather, anything can and will happen. There are life-changing storms in *Robinson Crusoe* and *A High Wind in Jamaica*, still favorite books of his. He recalls the opening lines of Walter Lord's *A Night to Remember*: "High in the crows nest of the New White Star liner *Titanic*, Lookout Frederick Fleet peered into a dazzling night. It was calm, clear, and bitterly cold. There was no moon, but the cloudless sky blazed with stars. The Atlantic was like polished plate glass; people later said they had never seen it so smooth."

Those poor, doomed passengers. It is a wonder to him that a reader, especially the reader of biography who already knows how the particular story ends, reads on anyway, as though through the sheer force of engagement, the outcome will be different. He sneaks into the silent kitchen to grab an apple, and sneaks out again before anyone sees him.

"It was an inauspicious journey," he writes, upping the pressure with foreshadowing. Apple juice makes his fingers sticky on the keys, forcing him to type more emphatically. "The living and the dying were filled with brandy, and for their amusement, a drunken monkey . . . tottered and screeched in the rigging."

He describes how twenty-seven days out of San Francisco, the steamer arrived in New York: "Clemens breathed in the biting air on the upper deck as his ship . . . crushed its way through the ice toward Castle Island and the city that lay north of it, a forest of church steeples palisaded by masts."

As Twain glances over his shoulder, the past recedes, and my father feels the excitement that comes from knowing more than Twain does at this moment: what the man's expansive future holds, how he will triumph, suffer, triumph again, experience fulfillment as well as disillusionment, love, bankruptcy, and terrible grief and loneliness. This is the tension and regeneration, this is Twain's conflicted and driven self, that will fuel the story he is so close to completing.

Joe sways in his chair and hears the ice cracking under the ship. He hears his wife at the front door talking to the delivery man: potatoes, spring asparagus, a roasting chicken. Dinner. Yes, *this*, he thinks. *This* is how you tell a story. He's done his research and reading, and every day he understands just a little bit better that writing a biography is not just a matter of gathering information and laying it out on the page. Facts are the stones of structures, but the stylistic and literary strategies of the dramatic storytelling he's doing are at the heart of the biography he hopes to write, one with the vivid force and arc of a novel.

"It comes down to story after all," he would explain years later in a lecture, "for you are committing a literary act if you take biography as seriously as it deserves to be taken."

It's been a good day of writing for him. He has taken his readers on a seasick voyage, warned them to duck those drunk monkeys, imagine what *palisaded* looks like, and appreciate the virility of a ship crushing through ice. He knows how Twain's story ends, just as I know how my father's does, yet we are both suspended, as Twain was on the deck of that sidewheeler facing east, in that moment when we still believe that anything can happen. To write is to move between what you already know and what you still need to discover.

The summer before my father's book was published, when I was six, we stayed in an English countryside rental called the oast house. He set up his study in the oast itself, a circular brick structure that had been used for drying hops. It was a fantastical and airy space, topped with a party-hat of a roof, and he spent his days in there going over his galley proofs, the long slippery pages hanging off the edge of the desk like pale tongues. We were not allowed to bother him, but if I stood among the dogwood bushes outside, I could watch him through the open window.

The desk was in the middle of the otherwise empty white room with its stone floor, and when a breeze blew in, it lifted the pages. I knew what galley proofs were—the book before it was born—though the word *proof* confused me with its suggestion that my father was being asked to provide evidence that all those words and idea were his and were correct. I worried that if he wasn't careful, he'd get in trouble. He worked with a red pencil, sometimes reading out loud and listening to the sentences run the circumference of the room. Day after day, the proofs hanging over the desk's edge grew longer, but at an almost imperceptible rate. "I would not read the proof of one of my books for any fair & reasonable sum whatever, if I could get out of it," Twain had written in a letter to William D. Howells. Every morning, there were a million pages left for my father to go over and it seemed impossible that he would ever be done by the time we had to go home, and then what would happen? I held my breath.

My father reread what he had written. "[Twain] stopped work only when the sun set over the hills west of Florence, and then he had tea on the terrace under the olive trees, smoked his pipe, took his ease. He was enchanted with the view—'drunk with pleasure all the time'—but still he remembered other views."

Experience ricocheted between him and his subject as he assumed the same posture, looking for his ease. But at the end of the day, he was drawn and unsmiling, sensitive to light and our noise, sober with anxiety despite his gin and tonics, and he couldn't help remembering other, darker views. He scratched nonstop between his fingers, up and down his forearms, his cheeks, his legs, the back of his neck, his skin becoming increasingly inflamed and fissured and dotted with scabs.

That summer I had started exploring being alone and moving away from my sisters and my mother, even if it was only down the road fifty yards and still within sight of the house. In my equation, I was sure that the farther I got from where my father sat, the faster he could work, his pages would get done, and all would be saved. At the end of the road there was a wooden fence and posing cows. When I hung on the railing for the first time, a bull charged toward me from across the field. I was so terrified my eyes felt like they'd slammed against the back of my head, but soon I was also excited by my own risk-taking—and survival. The next day when the bull rushed me, I wasn't so quick to back away from the fence, which after all was there to separate us. This animal and I had an understanding, I decided; he wouldn't hurt me because he knew me and knew what kind of girl I was—quiet, sensitive, appreciative. I smelled everything about him, and saw myself reflected in his glassy black eye.

One evening a few days before we left, I asked my father to walk with me to the end of the road. I always knew when his head was somewhere else and I felt myself disappearing in his presence, but as the thin English light grew indigo ahead of us on the road, he began to enjoy the walk. We stopped to throw pebbles at an empty metal drum and swat at the bugs. When we reached the fence, as always, the bull came charging across the field, the width of his chest like a truck, the smirk of his horns aimed right at us. His thunderous steps rose through my bones in a way I hadn't felt before; anticipation of this moment had thinned out my bravery. My father yanked me hard off the fence. My glasses fell onto the dusty road, but I could still see that he was furious, red-faced, stuttering. Didn't I see how dangerous this was? he demanded. What a stupid, stupid thing I'd done. This was an animal; it didn't have feelings about people, and it was not my friend. "He could have killed you," he said.

His touch was so rare that the weight of his hands lingered on my shoulders, my animal romance dispelled, as we started back toward the house. "Now the book was about to go to press, and as [Twain] handed it over . . . he made some emotionally charged connections between the work he had done and the life he saw before him," my father had written, and I knew whispering Twain was with us that night on that English road, the house already disappearing in the dark in front of us.

My father hadn't been able to sleep that summer. He was plagued by nightmares and his traitorous skin, and when we returned to Cambridge, he was quickly admitted to Mass General Hospital with an acute flare-up of his eczema, caused, Dr. Fitzpatrick said, by anxiety over finishing his book. Or more specifically, anxiety over what might and might not happen to the book—and to him—once it was published. Even if he could have envisioned then the reception his book would receive, how it would be the start of a long and enviable career, and how seemingly overnight (though it was never overnight, not after years and years of work, sentence by sentence, word by word) he would enjoy great success and admiration, he wouldn't have been soothed. He needed to collapse. The book had taken everything out of him in the way no other book he wrote ever would again.

A skin disease is a problem of self-presentation and a new book is not all that different; they both expose much of what we've struggled to keep inside. With the imminent release of *Mr. Clemens and Mark Twain*, Joe had scratched to shed his old skin and inhabit a new one. With the release of my first book, I'd suffered a similar flare-up of my skin. That charging English bull had contained the specter of disaster for him, for his future lying in typescript in that empty round room, for my future, too.

How could he have known that one day, almost six decades after that summer of worry, almost six decades after the book had been published, I would receive an email that made me imagine barging into his study, no knocking, no permission needed now, to find him alive in there once again.

"Dear Prof. Kaplan," I read, though I am no professor. "How wonderful to learn from Quarry Farm that you are writing a bio of your father! As you know, his biography of Mark Twain was a landmark in the field."

The email's author, Taylor Roberts of Toronto, had seen that I had been named a Mark Twain Fellow by the Center for Mark Twain Studies, and that I would be spending two weeks at Quarry Farm in Elmira, New York, where Twain and his family had spent many summers and where Twain had been enormously productive, writing among other things, *The Adventures of Huckleberry Finn*. (Quarry Farm had belonged Twain's father-in-law, and later it was given, along with Twain's famous octagonal study, to Elmira College and overseen by the Center for Mark Twain Studies. During my time there, as the sole occupant of the house, I wrote in Twain's rooms, ate at his kitchen table, slept and paced in his rooms, and dreamed myself into another time. On my first night sleeping under Twain's roof, a massive storm broke the end of the summer heat, and a cat appeared miraculously on the ledge outside my second-story window, soaked and mewling. I couldn't understand how it had gotten up there, or how it was gone in the next flash of lightning, only to appear every late afternoon after that to wind around my legs as I sat in Twain's rocking chair on the stone veranda that looked out over the Chemung River Valley. Could my father ever have imagined *this?*)

Perhaps I would be interested to see, Mr. Roberts writes, a behind-the-scenes movie clip he'd attached: *Roddy McDowall Planet of the Apes Home Movies 1967 Part 1 of 3.* He suggests I pay particular attention at about the three-minute mark.

My father is intrigued: Where can this possibly be going?

At the start of the clip, which I play for him on my laptop, the 20th Century Fox logo appears on a door, then British actor Maurice Evans, who plays Dr. Zaius, sits at a dressing table in full ape costume with a blond flip wig, smoking a cigarette. He turns to the camera, smiles as well as he can in his ape mask, then blows smoke out of the side of his mouth, all of this accompanied by the movie's ominously pounding soundtrack. I am reminded of how terrified I was of the movie when I first saw it. Scenes of moviemaking and set-building follow, crews hauling equipment, apes mingling in the bright sun, then a couple of actors in full ape getup in dark shirts and khaki pants sitting in director's chairs on a break in the shade. One of the apes, in black-rimmed glasses, is reading, his furry ape hands holding open the covers of a thick hardcover book, one beefy ape finger delicately turning the page. The book is *Mr. Clemens and Mark Twain*.

"This would have been 1967," Mr. Roberts adds in his email, "when your dad's book would have been hot off the press." To hear him refer to Joe as my "dad" is still startling and delightful, the taboo of that name as fresh as ever.

Joe adores this, and we play the clip several more times, always laughing at the moment when the book appears clasped in simian fingers.

"That's just wonderful," he says, over and over, reminding me of his capacity for pleasure and gratitude, for delight in the unexpected and the incongruent, and for finding ourselves in hands we never imagined would hold us.

Nine

Memory and Aspiration

•

*"Livy sleeps, imagination and memory awake
and seek out the past. She is a flesh-and-blood
wife, but she is also a guiding principle, a sym-
bolic figure he invests with its own power to select and purify."*

It's a December morning, and my father is deep into the writing of his book. Francis Avenue is buried and muffled from
last night's huge snowstorm and he plans to stuff me and Susanna into snowsuits later and pull us on a sled with metal
runners down the middle of the unplowed street. Storms have
always given him license to goof off a bit; he adores the sanc-
tioned aggression of snowball fights. First, though, in the
blinding light, he intends to write about Twain and Olivia
Langdon—Livy—the woman who would become his wife.
He wants to write their love story, while I already know that
he will never write his own, that perhaps he can't, and that I
will write it for him.

He glances out the window and sees his neighbor bundled

in a tweed jacket, a plaid scarf, and deerstalker hat. The man may be an esteemed historian, but he's useless with a shovel, blinking against the whiteout as he wages a battle between intention and execution, same as the writer's battle. When a clod of snow slides from the slate roof and lands with a heavy thud just beyond his study window, rattling the bare lilac bushes, my father moves from the present moment to the past and types, "[Twain's] first meetings with [Livy] caressed and quickened memory and aspiration." Caressed and quickened memory and aspiration. A lot packed into that sentence, but he's sure those are the right words. He is unaware that what and how he writes about another man's story of love is bolstered and informed by his own still unwritten one, and how it will remain there for me to find and tell so many years later.

Twain had said, "I never, never expected to be the hero of a romance in real life as unlooked for and unexpected as the wildest of them," and my father doesn't hear the resonance in his own life as I do. After all, I know he was directionless, alone, melancholy, and so cavalier about women until he met my mother. He turns to look at pictures of her above the fireplace and then back to his desk where tokens are lined up like a rebus coding their private past and shared sense of the future: a coin they found on their honeymoon, a glass Rotary International paperweight my mother nicked from her father's desk for him, a khaki-colored rectangular gum eraser bought in a London stationery store. (Mistakes will be made.)

He returns to his typewriter to describe Twain's first glimpse of Livy years before he was to marry her: "by a chance occurrence that compounded the deepest personal commitment with the almost comically trivial, he saw the grave and delicate face of Olivia Langdon" in an ivory miniature.

Calling this chance occurrence "almost comically trivial" exposes my young father's skittishness about buying too heavily into legends of love, in spite of those trinkets on his desk. When I read in *Back Then* his description of how he blushed when one day he passed the woman on the street who would later become his wife—"She wore a little gray suede hat and a rosy red wool coat, and she had a rosy aura"—his attention to the indelible details of this crosswalk encounter is no more "comically trivial" than Twain's encounter with the ivory miniature, but he can't see this. His memoirist's voice remains distant still, unruffled, unwilling to invite the reader in. With an intellectual and cool stance and insistence on maintaining that certain empathetic distance, it's as though he's writing about himself as the subject of a biography.

When Mark Twain came to New York in 1867 at age thirty-two, he was without "binding commitment to place or social identity." When my father at twenty-one returned to New York in 1947, having left graduate school at Harvard (or been asked to leave), he also found himself without work, commitment, identity, or any sense of what he might do with his life. Money his father had left him enabled the lassitude, but he woke every morning, his skin on fire, considering the possibility that he might never leave a mark—or even a faint footprint—on the world. In these moments of his first consciousness, I detect glimmers of an impulse to write as a way to find his place, but he didn't know yet that love could lead him there.

He roamed New York City ("Manhattan's Streets I Saunter'd, Pondering," Whitman wrote), and when he could work up the courage to counter his social insecurity, he went to parties thrown by his friends in publishing that were full of awe-inspiring guests: Robert Penn Warren, Somerset Maugham, Dame Edith Sitwell, Norman Mailer, William Faulkner, Richard Yates. If all that literary star power left him feeling even more adrift and ghostly, he discovered at these parties that the way women were drawn to him, this tall cipher with the shy smile and the unspoken history, this character worthy of a novel I could write, made him feel, at least for the moment, found.

My father was uncharacteristically revealing about his romantic past, and my sisters and I grew up hearing his stories, told with wistfulness and pride, about his many girlfriends during these wandering years. He said that on some days he'd slept with one woman in the morning and another in the afternoon before scurrying off to his shrink appointment after a hastily downed sandwich at a lunch counter. His tone always suggested to me that he'd pulled one over on the shrink, leaving me to wonder what he thought the whole venture of emotional reckoning and exploration (he would spend almost five years in psychoanalysis) had or had not achieved. During those years, he hungered for affection and women loved him like a lost boy, offering him plenty of existence-confirming solace in spite of what he later called his "faithless and self-serving behavior." The entanglements kept him in their eddies, and he had no interest in swimming in calmer waters just then; he wouldn't have known how anyway.

I was twelve when he told us how one of his girlfriends had called him from her hotel room on her wedding night while her new husband was in the bathroom brushing his teeth. My mother enjoyed the story, my father's allure apparently so great it pierced even the honeymoon suite. But I felt all he'd given up to be with us and didn't want to know any of it any more than I wanted to watch my parents at the end of the table deep kiss and paw each other, a nightly performance that flung me out of my own body.

Today, though, the honeymoon story serves to help me write him as a romantic itinerant experiencing a depth of loneliness that the breezy retelling of those tales hid, one that stops him one desperate January night on a New York street corner outside a woman's apartment. He can't remember her name or even what she looks like. Aimlessness is stagnation, and he is stuck. What will he do with his life? Who will see it unfold with him? He has no home, no work, no place in the world. Slush seeps through his shoes and socks, wets the backs of his pant legs. He doesn't know which way to go, but his eyes are just beginning to open up to who he might become once he's found the woman with whom he will hold himself to account through the agency of love and commitment.

"I want to get located in life," Twain had said before marriage, my father adding that "[he] had known Whitman's open road long enough, and what he wanted was home." (In a moment of prescience about his future work, my father closed the circle with his two biographical subjects in one authorial breath.)

In this mood, my father suggests, "there begins to emerge the crucial web of motives and conditions by which [Twain] would flourish as a writer." Unaware of the resonance still, he makes a telling and self-referential leap in suggesting a critical association between marriage's promise of land after years at sea, and the writer's ability to discover his material and get down to work.

Marriage is a deliberate life and it is place; if all goes well, it *is* home. For the writer, home is the paper and pen and the idea, another day, the chair, the desk, the closed door, and the reassurance that there is someone else on the other side of it when he is ready to emerge. "The fountains of my great deep are broken up," Twain had written after his wedding to Livy. My father might even use Twain's word *drowsing* again to describe the dreamlike quality of those early days of marriage with my mother when he could also "conjure up an image of childhood purified by the years." My father knew that with its presumption of goodness and stability, marriage offered a way to make use of the storms without being swept away in them, to draw on the energy and productive tension between the present moment and the past that he can never fully leave behind.

In drawing a link between love and work, my father remembered his own emerging notion that marrying my mother and living in the promise of deep care and loving protection might actually free him to find identity and place, accountability and probity, and his way to leave that terrible winter corner and arrive at this very moment when he pushes back from his desk after a good day of writing and calls to me and my sister to get our coats on, we're going out.

My mother and Livy, both pampered and privileged young women, chose to wed the men they weren't supposed to and found a way to break away from rigid parents and rigid expectations. "As a prospective son-in-law, when Annie first told [her parents] about me," my father wrote in *Back Then*, ". . . [they] probably would have preferred a (high-caste) Hindu to a Jew, Harvard apart, from the other side of Central Park. Their first response to a potential wrenching of their social order was plain disbelief. 'You must be joking!'"

Livy's parents were equally as unenthusiastic at the prospect of Twain marrying their daughter. My father could poke fun at the small-minded elitism and caste warfare of these in-laws because he—and Twain—had ultimately prevailed, but winning them over hadn't been easy and required the presentation of a more coherent and directed self both men saw could be made possible through love.

My father wrote that before marriage, Twain had visited Livy in her father's brownstone mansion in Elmira: "Three sets of iron gates, baronially clanging when they opened or shut, gave entrance to grounds covering a city block."

In his using the finicky word *baronially*, I see my father matching Twain footstep for footstep, breaking into a cold, itchy sweat as he is also ushered into his future in-laws' mahogany-rich foyer, this one on New York's Upper East

Side. My father and Twain stand in this lily-scented world, both of them recognizing what Twain called "that odor of sanctity which comes with cash." Acceptance wasn't going to be easy for either man. As a Jew of Eastern European descent attempting to join my mother's family of German Jews, my father wrote about a dinner with his daunting future in-laws: "Placed with my back to an active fireplace, I could as well have been a planked shad ready to be deboned. Whether placing me close to a pile of burning logs, to roast there like a heretic, was mischief or accident I couldn't tell." I detect his pride in his having broken into the castle, but it came with an awareness of being an outsider ready for the stake.

Livy's parents had requested letters of reference for Twain—their own form of burning logs. Livy's mother had especially deep doubts about him and his ability to alter his rough ways. My father's impatience with her narrow-mindedness and classism is unbridled and personal—"Such were the terms of a character investigation which was as remarkable for its naïveté as for the amount of sheer discredit it collected"—as it was with his own future in-laws.

My father claimed he was "fond" of his in-laws, a word so damning coming from him that it requires collusion on my part to see its upside. When he writes about Twain's father-in-law, Jervis Langdon, a successful coal and iron monopolist, I hear the same circumspection he uses to write about his own father-in-law, Edward L. Bernays. In his description of Langdon as unfettered "by the conflict between private and business morality" are echoes of his feelings about my grandfather who applied some of his uncle Sigmund's theories to this new profession of public relations where the public's unconscious could be influenced and guided without them being aware it was happening.

Eddie, as everyone called him, fascinated and repelled my father, a man whose rapacity in business sometimes seemed conveniently blind to ethical considerations. In one inspired campaign for the American Tobacco Company in 1928, Eddie persuaded women to reject the stigma of smoking in public and light up "torches of freedom" as they marched in New York's Easter Parade. My mother's nonstop war against smoking—mine in particular—was in reaction to her father's contribution to smoking's death toll. We joked at home in a way that spoke to our deep unease about his work and influence that my grandfather would have taken Hitler on as a client if he'd been asked, and we called public relations "the dark side of advertising." "His unconscious was nobody's business, not even his own," my father said about him with Twainian dexterity.

On weekends, we went to my grandparents' house for lunch. They had moved from New York to Cambridge in the 1950s, where my mother's sister and her family already lived, into a large and chilly house just off Brattle Street, which my grandfather had deemed the best address in the city. The house was filled with faded rugs, art, and objects. Eddie had once bought a mummy of an Egyptian princess in a glass box at an auction just because he could and kept it in his living room until my grandmother Doris made him take it to the office. Awards and plaques, glass obelisks, engraved silver bowls, framed proclamations, photographs, all attesting to my grandfather's importance and connections were in evidence everywhere.

Barrel shaped and always in a jacket and tie, Eddie held forth from the velvet couch, name-dropping and dispensing unasked-for advice, supremely self-confident in understanding how life should play out for everyone else. The wall of books behind him included the many he'd written, as well as my grandmother's *A Wife Is Many Women*, a title that should come with a wink given her subjugation to her husband. Perhaps a publicity stunt designed to garner attention in the newspapers, she was the first married American woman to have a passport issued in her maiden name. That she was held up by my grandfather as a pioneer in women's rights felt like one of the construction paper animals we made to represent ourselves in first grade and pinned to our shirts; just because I wore a blue bird didn't mean I was one. She radiated a dislike for me and a deep unhappiness, and I tried to stay out of her sightline as she sat on the edge of her chair, her black purse on her lap as though it contained an escape she might use one day. Or a tissue she might need to dab at her disappointed eye.

While my father had his own conflicted feelings about being Jewish, and had no use for the conventions of religious membership, particularly the orthodoxy of his parents' Judaism, my grandfather's open and vigorous anti-Semitism infuriated him as it cut down everyone and everything my father had come from. My father's gentle demeanor hid a well of indignation, and I sometimes witnessed him at a lunch that had been ordered from a Jewish deli, wield his intellectual acrobatics and sarcasm to make my grandfather trip over his own snobbery and moralism. He was less brave with my icy grandmother who sat motionless in her chair, while my mother, in a display of her vulnerability and deep insecurity that was so often masked, as it was for my father, looked like a child still falling short of approval and love.

My mother said her mother never told her she loved her, never kissed or hugged her. I wasn't sure if this was an admission or a warning. There had been cherry trees in my grandparents' backyard, scratchy, malformed, and briefly bright with their flowering. They were the only things I ever heard my grandmother say she liked, and after they succumbed to disease and had to be yanked out, she would sit in the screened porch and sigh at the ghosts of their promise. It was a house full of the spoils and expectation of success and stature, but it was a house empty of affection.

Like Twain, who in marrying into the Langdon family had "suffered something like rootburn from his transplanting," my father knew my mother's family would always be foreign soil to him, always to some degree inhospitable to his roots, so he and my mother planted their own. When we returned home midafternoon from one of these visits to my grandparents', the dog was waiting in the front hall, the coffee cups were still on the counter from breakfast, and life welcomed us back. My sisters and I took off our shoes and scattered, and my father was especially solicitous of my mother on those days, not immediately going in to his study. He might agree to play a game of Scrabble with her at the kitchen table with the radio on in the background, or invite her to sit in the chair next to his desk and read to her, and by dinnertime, soothed by his loyalty and affection, and by their shared promise to never abandon the other, she would have returned to her self.

"Soon after Annie and I became engaged," my father wrote in *Back Then*, "a psychologist we met at a party told us we were the worst imaginable marital risk. Each of us was the younger sibling in a family of two same-sex offspring, and younger siblings, he said, being as a rule demanding, dependent, and self-centered from infancy on, proved unable to meet the needs of similarly disadvantaged partners in marriage."

Half a century later, the psychologist might have still been right on the "similarly disadvantaged" front, but his mistake was in thinking that their needs were competitive instead of complementary. In the love story I tell, it is out of luck or some profound recognition of their opposing shortcomings and strengths that they made the right match.

Today my father and I are in Cape Cod Bay together on an imagined July afternoon. He's an eighty-seven-year-old sinewy and sick Parkinsonian paddler in his red kayak while I swim alongside and struggle to keep up. He's wearing a bathing suit and a T-shirt that says *Marriage is so gay*. He's been done with writing biography for a while. His stint as general editor of *Bartlett's Familiar Quotations* is long over, and his last book, *When the Astors Owned New York*, was published a few years earlier. He was too tired to do much to promote it beyond a few readings here and there. For a while, he's been searching for a new writing project, starting and abandoning ideas during those long hours he still spends in his summer study. He's lost again, his younger self reappearing as if to say all that business of life's uncertainty is still waiting for its due.

"Look at this," he says, lifting up a long spongy web of seaweed on his oar. "Too bad you can't eat the stuff."

He is a hedonist when it comes to the water, and he imagines how he might describe it, still concerned with how to transform beauty into language. I want my father to be working again because he fades when he isn't, and on this kayak outing of ours, it's his love I want him to write about. But first I tell him that as I read his book, it's Twain's relationship with Livy that has the strongest pulse and ensures that everything else comes fully to life. Their story eases regret and awakens hope, stands up against disappointment and even death, and through reading about how he wrote about it, despite all his squeamishness about anything tendrilled with sentiment, I have discovered his.

I remind him of how he wrote about Twain, a determined suitor still at that point, leaving Elmira one night where he'd gone to call on Livy. Twain had called it a "lucky accident" when he'd fallen into a gutter when a horse startled and had to be carried back to her house. "It was one of those episodes in his life which . . . had the shape of daydream to begin with and which he made part of his own mythology." I tell him how I strung his own lucky accidents and episodes—the chance crosswalk encounter with the woman in the rosy red wool coat—together into the story that saved him.

He blushes, though it could just be the sun pinking his cheeks. He returns the seaweed to the bay and reminds me of the house rules about writing biography. "You can't just put thoughts in my head as though I'm one of your characters. You can't just make things up and call it true because it's convenient and fits the story you've decided you want to tell. Would you like me to do that to you?"

"Actually, yes," I say. I would love to know what story he would tell about me.

He never talked to his three daughters about love, about heartbreak, divorce, betrayal, what to want or accept or walk away from. He was always polite but wary of his sons-in-law. I don't know if he thinks I'm happy in my marriage, or if he thinks about it at all, if he realizes at this moment that I also began to write with any seriousness when I fell in love over thirty years ago and found a way and place to put the things I felt and saw and was moved by. That this is my love story that led me to today. (On the morning of my wedding, he only asked if I knew what the bride's second biggest disappointment was after Niagara Falls.)

Hanging on to the side of the kayak, I tell him that I heard yesterday from an old friend of mine who'd just run into her ex-husband. About the history of their marriage, she'd said, "He was an easy man to be married to and an easy man to be divorced from." I tell him that her line is a reminder to me that the stories we tell shift to accommodate who we are and what we want at any moment, that they are always re-creations, wishful or dooming concoctions, and that my friend had not been quite so even-handed about her husband when she was still married to him. Even our diaries and journals—even his notes I've uncovered—those repositories of the kind of raw and flawed gems we swear we'll never show anyone, not even when we're dead, are still only flashes of the moment, and every page should end with *Ask me how I feel about this tomorrow.*

After he returns the kayak to the shore, he swims far out, reminding me of how he had described Whitman: "From his boyhood along the Atlantic shore, Whitman remembered the sea whispering to him, 'the low and delicious word death, and again, death, death, death . . . Cradled, rocked and drowsing, his body rolling silently to and fro in the heave of the water,' he lay suspended between the depths and the light, between the unconscious and the world of necessity." I want again to tell him to try writing about himself, that to finally tell his own story with all its pain and pleasure, strength and fragility, feeling and doubt, will keep him from fading, but I know that he won't be alive by the following summer. So I've written it for both of us.

The love story has no burden of honesty, we write it as we want. Its gestures and observations are always prescient and animated by hindsight, its details lean toward the desired effect. It is the truest kind of fiction, a truth powered in part by the fear of losing the thing we hope to have forever.

Ten

Insider / Outsider

•

*"In Nook Farm, a tiny, coherent, and influen-
tial community nesting in the larger structure of
Hartford, [Twain] achieved a crucial balance of
inner imperatives and outer pressures that led to
the most productive period of his life."*

Like Nook Farm in Hartford that embraced Twain among its
elite, Francis Avenue regarded itself as a hotbed of intellectual
pursuit and accomplishment, where originality and grinding
hard work prevailed. With its large and gently faded houses,
it was, as described in *The Washington Post*, "a street of un-
ostentatious, comfortable assumption." When my father, still
a fresh and unvetted resident, first wrote that Twain "needed
'a complex social machinery' to set him in motion," he might
have been hoping that the same would prove true for him
some day on the street, even as he was familiar with his own
mixed feelings about belonging to anything.

The neighborhood was full of writers, scientists, Nobel

Prize winners, diplomats, composers, artists, well-known thinkers and scholars, some of whom came and went with the new academic year. The economist and presidential adviser John Kenneth Galbraith, who lived a few houses down, had said, "On most streets what determines whether you can buy a house is how much it costs; here it's how many books you've written." The professor two doors over had a barn door in his basement that had belonged to Melville. The man across the street, an "eminent" sociologist (I knew the tag before I knew what it meant) and descendant of two Adams presidents, had a vestigial tail, or so I'd been told, and I lived in hope of someday spotting it when he bent to pick up his newspapers from the front walk. Julia Child lived over one corner of our back fence, and one afternoon she'd invited me into her kitchen to taste something from a wooden spoon. I'd seen her hoist her husband, Paul, into a tree so he could rescue a cat caught on a branch. William James's house was over another part of the back fence, as was the house where e. e. cummings had been born. Joe had noted that the New England literati of another era had worked up in Twain not awe, "but a certain tempered amusement. 'Why, you couldn't stand on your front porch and fire off your revolver without bringing down a two-volumer.'" He must have felt the same tempered amusement when he stood on his own front porch, breathed in the street's atmosphere, and detected its electric zing thrown off by the many big brains working devotedly behind closed doors. My father had told me that once out on a walk not long after the critical success of his book, a neighbor had stopped him on the street and said about his National

Book Award, "That's all very well, but what are you going to do for an encore?"

It was not a street of neighborly barbecues, coolers of six-packs, plastic pools, games of tag, toys left out on walkways, or even children's voices. There was a hush necessary to work that I knew wasn't to be disturbed. Many houses on the street turned out their lights on Halloween; one professor and his wife hired someone every year to dole out candy while they lurked in the background, eager for the siege to end. One year, my sisters and I rang the bell of a house around the block, and a man in silk tunic and pants opened the door. (Later we would learn that he was a visiting scholar from India at Harvard for the year.) He was confused by three girls in homemade costumes, so we explained to him what Halloween was about. He had no candy, he was sorry to say, but he took us into a pantry off the kitchen and gave us a tin of Camembert cheese, a sleeve of English biscuits, and a jar of bitter marmalade.

There were other children on the street, but we didn't play together, and we regarded each other with some suspicion and a mutually assumed understanding of what life was like inside, as though we were mirroring the adults. One girl told me that in her house, if she wanted to talk to her father, she had to make an appointment to see him. I had watched as an older boy dropped his clothes, one piece at a time, out of his bedroom window so that shirts and underwear and sneakers flew by his father working at a desk in the room below, the man barely looking up as though it had only been a bird's shadow passing by. Last year, I heard from a woman who had lived across the street when we were young. My father was notable among the other fathers for playing Frisbee with us, she told me, and she'd watched wistfully as he stood on one side of the street, my sisters and I on the other, the dog sauntering between the two until one day a car came racing down the wrong way and hit her.

At the far end of the block, where Harvard buildings staked their claim and influence, the ROTC building squatted incongruously at the back of a parking lot where we could ride bikes on the weekend. I thought its ugly, low-slung structure and stingy windows covered by wire was its own punishment for existing at all, and to even touch its red asphalt shingles was to be on the wrong side of the Vietnam War. In 1970, when Harvard SDS students planned to march down our street and Divinity Avenue to take over the building, my parents shipped us off to my aunt's house across town for safety. First, though, they'd had us draw a giant peace sign on a bed sheet to hang from the front door so the protestors would pass us by. After the march, the sheet went back into the closet, and would from time to time appear on my bed where I slept under the fading ink memory. Three years earlier, my father had donated his Pulitzer Prize money to the American Friends Service Committee. He might just as well have written his statement about "honoring the American tradition of constructive consent that Twain served so nobly" in chalk in the middle of the street for the students to march over.

Harvard Divinity School was next to the ROTC building and around the corner from Harvard Hillel, where out of some diluted sense of obligation to the religion they'd been born into, my parents had sent us very briefly to Hebrew school. With their mixed feelings about being part of anything prescribed and their already tepid interest in this form of education, we lasted only a few months. It had been painful for me to sit in a room with kids my age, know nothing that they did, and feel acutely that I didn't belong. I felt no more comfortable when I sang carols at my private school's Christmas assembly, and worried that some celestial punishment for this crime would be visited on me. I had adopted my parents' defensive stance against feeling like an outsider, but mine was cloaked in shyness. The allure of belonging was intense, but the exposure of fraud it might uncover was equally powerful, and I couldn't pass the Hillel building after quitting Hebrew school without a deep sense of confusion.

The cyclotron (Cambridge Electron Accelerator), which was just beyond the Divinity School, exploded on the night of July 5, 1965, with a tremendous, bed-shaking boom. From up and down the street neighbors came out of their houses in nightgowns and pajamas and slippers to watch the commotion and talk as though they were at a cocktail party or a faculty reception. Two weeks later, when a student who had been working in the cyclotron died of injuries sustained in the explosion, my parents discussed over breakfast the irony of an atom smasher living cheek to jowl with a divinity school. I had always been sure that there was something divinely charged, and apparently fatally overcharged, about that end of the street, and when I was there, I obeyed a cosmic law against goofing around or making too much noise.

The sidewalks opposite the Divinity School were littered with oily brown chestnuts in the fall that to this day retain for me a spiritual glow, as though they drop only in pious places. My father stooped to collect them on our walks and always had one or two in his pocket that he was ready to give to someone as a spontaneous present. He never explained this simple gift to the receiver, the chestnut's mysterious beauty and my father's gesture of affection explanation enough.

Every spring, John Kenneth Galbraith's large front yard was a riot of daffodils, and later in the season it hosted a riot of dignitaries, celebrities, and important people who attended his annual Harvard commencement afternoon garden party. It would be seven years after they moved to Francis Avenue, and not until the publication and recognition of my father's book, that my parents received an invitation from any neighbor, and when their garden party invitation finally arrived, it was evidence to them that they'd made it, made something, made a name on their own terms and without the institutional affiliations that seemed stamped across the foreheads and chests of so many others. (Acknowledgment of my mother's accomplishments would always be slower and much less generous.) For days before the party, my parents discussed what they would wear and who might be there, and for days after, they replayed the highlights and dramas of the famous and the fatuous. Police and the press lined the street on the afternoon of the party, limos pulled up to deliver their luminaries, others wandered over from commencement activities in Harvard Yard's tercentenary theater, and my sisters and I, sitting barefoot on our front steps, watched the parade and felt as though we lived at the center of the universe.

But even as my father walked four houses down to the party, the scent of his cologne trailing after him, even as he adjusted his flowery Liberty of London tie while all the other men wore striped ones, even as he and my mother whispered together, as he looked back at us, I could see that ambivalence and nerves accompanied him. His friend Annie Dillard described him as "original in his judgments, and not limited by reputation, schools, class, consensus. None of this 'one-of-us' stuff." He was no forward-looking or reverse snob, he was always judging himself, but he had to wonder, on those occasions, who let me in? And now that I'm in, is this really where I want to be?

One year, my sisters and I set up a lemonade stand on the sidewalk, cajoling dimes out of people on their way to the party, and when my father came out of our house, he lingered too long on our side of the sticky table. He was very much an insider by all external standards—his literary stature and success, this house on Francis Avenue—but this remove was a more comfortable place, an expression of self-reliance and a fiercely protected independence, and my father's lifelong doubt of his own worthiness. On that day, despite all the fanfare and excitement of the party down the street and how hard my father had worked to get there, it was a thrilling moment for me to see that he'd rather take off his tie and jacket and watch the procession from the sidelines with us.

"The public personality of Mark Twain, the eccentric demon born of the needs, aggressions, and reticences of Sam Clemens, was still in flux, no longer the simple bookish observer and teller of tall stories but becoming a man of the world now, ironic, polished, and confident," my father wrote. Like the Twain he had come to know, my father became increasingly adept at navigating the conflicting feelings of the outsider who finds himself a reluctant insider.

The resulting inner conflict armed my father with humor's many defenses. "'Weapon,' 'blast,' 'assault'—these are some of Mark Twain's ways of nailing down the essential action of humor," he wrote, recognizing the language of battle. A few years after the Twain book was published, he was invited to speak to a professional organization of psychiatrists in Boston about the art of biography. He had been nervous talking to this group with their collective self-seriousness. A whole room of shrinks staring back at him? Who wouldn't start sweating and joking away the discomfort by hovering somewhere between the taboo and the permissible. He blotted his face with the handkerchief he always carried. He cleared his throat and then cleared it again. The whole setup was starting to feel like a blood sport, and like Twain under social pressure, he could play the false naïf, tease and enchant, and respond "with a troubled mingling of gratitude, residual veneration, mockery, and barely disguised hostility, all contained within a mild hoax." When it was time for questions, a woman in the audience stood and asked him how he saw Twain's life "vis-à-vis the oral triad." He saw an opportunity for a deliberate misunderstanding of the question, for the power of humor to disarm. Without missing a beat, he answered, "The only oral triad I know is bacon, lettuce, and tomato."

I imagine that everyone in that room of shrinks was left unsure about whether my father's joke was meant to delight, repel, charm, tease, or mock them. I often couldn't tell myself. When he wrote about Twain's indelicate humor, his delight at standing in front of an ancient bust and asking, "Is he dead?" my father asserted that this was Twain's "way of rejecting the past, the uncomfortable emotions of outsideness and awe."

Hiding behind his cleverness and determined to deflect any line of self-questioning, Joe's humor seemed, too, to shield his own raw nerve endings.

Until adulthood, bacon had always been a forbidden food for my father; at home, I'd seen him devour it. To eat a BLT, then, was not simply a delight but a mouthwatering assertion of agency. Those collected psychiatrists, had they not been so disarmed by the exquisitely agile silliness of his answer, might have pointed this out to him.

After he won his second National Book Award in 1981, my father was invited to become a member of the Tavern Club, considered to be the top social and business club in Boston, a place according to my mother that a man would kill his mother-in-law to get into. The only club my father had ever joined with enthusiasm was the Cambridge Skating Club, where in the winter he would skate across the bumpy surface of the flooded tennis courts with his hands behind his back and a scarf around his neck, a Semitic Hans Brinker.

It was no ambition of his to become a member, but he accepted the offer, maybe out of flattery or envy of other men's senses of rootedness and belonging. From the beginning, then, his joining the Tavern Club seemed a doomed fit, and once a month he attempted to play the role of member by putting on a suit, polishing his shoes, and eating an overcooked dinner, usually sitting with a priest or one of the other social outliers. The next morning, I could see in his sheepishness at talking about it that the evening had depressed him. He never had a good time, didn't like all-male events, and was uncomfortable being one of the only—if not the only—Jewish member. Finally, when he declined the considerable pressure to take part in the annual Christmas play, he decided it was time to quit and wrote a letter of resignation. One of the members called and asked him to reconsider. When he wouldn't, the man said, "Young man, you're making the biggest mistake of your life," to which my father replied, "I certainly hope so."

There was almost nothing and no one deemed by my father too sacred to be poked fun of. This extended to children, especially his own, and teasing was a way to bypass the stickier parts of parenting. My disappointment could be turned into a frowning face he drew on the shell of my hard-boiled egg at breakfast. An extended joke that my real mother was a Pakistani woman who'd abandoned me at birth (no father was mentioned) became a kind of shorthand for my sensitivity, with echoes of his own absent mother. He convinced a friend of mine—we were about twelve years old—that there were traffic lights in the ocean so passing ships didn't run into each other. It sounded entirely plausible to me, but unlike my friend, I knew better than to admit this and had already learned to take the safer cynical stance. Her gullibility delighted my father, or maybe his delight was in how he could fire up the engines of her imagination, but in either case he didn't disabuse her of this idea that the vast sea had road rules.

When the young son of some friends, riding in the back seat of the car, asked my father why he held on to the handle above the door frame, Joe said it was to keep the roof from blowing off. He colored the white spots on the beagle with Magic Markers so the dog might wander the neighborhood in vivid green and pink, and when asked about it, he could tell people that she had been born like that.

Only my father's dermatologist at Mass General Hospital, Thomas Fitzpatrick, MD, was untouchable and sacred, and no jokes or jabs at him were ever made or allowed. The man doled out the kind of patience and care my father had never experienced in a doctor treating his skin condition. On the days of his appointments, my father set aside his work, put on a jacket and tie, and took the Red Line to the Charles Street station with all the solemnity of a holy pilgrimage to see this man who saw all of him, to whom he bared the torment of his body and psyche, to whom he was a single person, inside and out.

My mother's fear of exclusion, even as she too was an insider by all standards, led my parents to create their own literary and social universe with themselves at the core. By her account, for the briefest of moments, she and my father were the prom king and queen of Cambridge. "If there's a writer's community in Boston, they established it," the novelist James Carroll had said. "There was a period of about fifteen years when their house was the center of the writing life in Boston. Joe was the pillar, and Anne was the flame. Between the two of them they made a big difference in the life of the city."

They entertained often and there was an air of expectancy in the house on party days. My father was in charge of the booze and the glasses, and he walked to the liquor store on Kirkland Street in the afternoon to buy ice. He made giant pots of chili for the inner circle of guests who knew that if they stayed long enough, they might get fed. My mother set out cocktail napkins and bowls of peanuts. If any of the guests had a new book, my father made sure it was displayed on the coffee table. He was a generous and amusing host, skilled at making people feel welcome and listened to, and always more comfortable asking questions than answering them. Guests, particularly women, circled him, clutching their drinks and listened to one of his anecdotes, references, or dirty jokes. And like Twain who "shared [his neighbors'] . . . taste for entertaining each other and any eminence who happened to be passing through Hartford," my parents invited the eminences passing through Cambridge for a lecture, a reading, or a semester. They considered name-dropping a moral failing, but their parties on Francis Avenue drew the name-dropped through the front door—Seamus Heaney, John Irving, and Tim O'Brien, Edward Albee. Jessica Mitford, Richard Rhodes, Bella Abzug, William Styron, Wallace Shawn, and Deborah Eisenberg. Kurt Vonnegut spent the night on the living room couch after one of these parties and almost left out of frustration because my mother wouldn't stop bugging him about his smoking.

Some of the guests had their books reviewed in the *Times* (the clearest evidence of success) and occasionally even made money. But many others who came to the house would never ascend—or ascend for only the briefest of moments. I saw the panic of failure on their faces as they moved through these parties that were humid with literary glow and intense competition. Their books, like shards of their formerly hopeful selves, migrated to the piles in the small back rooms of our house, where the wallpaper peeled and the floors bleached in the sun. No book was ever thrown out, no matter how terrible it was.

There were writers in our house so knocked off course by initial success that they couldn't write another word, and those trying to come to terms with the fact that maybe they had only a single book in them. They might gaze at the brightest literary stars standing over by the bar and tossing back fistfuls of nuts and feel that their own careers, one book in, was already over.

The stakes were high at those parties that also included agents, publishers, critics, and journalists, and mention of a work in progress ran the risk of receiving a devastatingly blank look in return. If you knew what was good for you, you knew it was wiser not to talk about what you were working on. Did you dare show up after a trouncing review, or did you show up to prove it meant nothing? One writer who came regularly for years was so distraught at how badly his most recent book, which hadn't done well in reviews or sales, had been promoted by his publisher that he took the leather-bound copy of it, a gift from his editor, into his yard, hacked it up with an axe, put it in a mailer, and sent it back. The episode made my parents laugh uneasily; it wasn't so hard to imagine being driven to such extremes apparently, or fall from such heights, proof to me of how easy it was to lose your standing in this particular world. I always slowed my bike when I came to that man's fence, behind which I had frozen him in his jacket and tie, weapon aloft, tears on his cheeks, his book an innocent on the chopping block.

My father wrote that it was the interplay and balance of "inner imperatives and outer pressures" on Twain that created the most productive period of the man's life. Joe's own engagement with these conflictive forces—the writer's desire to be known and unknown at the same time, the public face and the "personal mythology," as he called it—fueled his work and insight into his subject. The place he was most profoundly his true self would always be in the writing. Ultimately, there was plenty of acceptance for my father on Francis Avenue and in the wide literary world and beyond. The outsider can also be the outsider of his own making, a useful pose of observation for a writer, and over the years my father's ambivalence found expression in quietly clear ways: painting the house in decidedly unneighborly colors, letting the garage list and rot to the point of near collapse, allowing the expansive backyard to become a jungle of weeds, and opening the door so the sweet dog Olive could wander through the neighborhood at night for as long and as far as she wanted, unleashed, alone, and dreamy.

Eleven

Brothers and Friends

•

*"In the matter of reliable 'references,' [Twain]
argued that only five people at most had ever
known him at all well and that he felt in entire sympathy with only two of them. One of the
two was his dead brother Henry; the other was
Livy."*

A few days after my father's obituary appeared in *The New
York Times*, a man who identified himself as my father's first
cousin called my parents' apartment.

"Sorry," I said, sniffing out a scam despite the frailty of his
voice, "but my father doesn't have any first cousins."

Joe's older brother and only sibling Howard had died more
than thirty years earlier, and as far as I knew, my father had
no other family beyond Howard's two sons who were close
to my age and whom I hadn't seen in decades. If there were
other relatives out there—including this cousin—I'd never
heard of them, and neither had my mother.

"Your father never talked about things like that," she said

vaguely, and added that she'd never asked. Years later, when I discovered that she also had relatives that I'd never known existed, including a cousin who lived only a few towns away, I felt just how tightly my parents had closed the circle around the two of them.

The man on the phone laughed, not unkindly, and told me that my father had many cousins, a whole lot of them in fact, and he went on to list them as though I might actually recognize these people if I heard their names. I imagined a farmhouse in a hazy summer field, insects buzzing over tall grass, and a wide porch filled with relatives who were eager to welcome me. That these conjured family members were more country folk from another century than urban Jew, more Florida, Missouri (birthplace of Mark Twain), than Manhattan (birthplace of Joe) was evidence of the confusion and wild incongruity of this news.

In the other room, my mother and sisters sifted through the condolence cards and cookies that had begun to arrive, and the air was weighted with their private inklings that the newly dead might walk in at any moment.

"You've never heard of me?" the cousin asked. "For a biographer, your father really had no interest in his own history, his own family, except Howard. We tried, but he didn't want us."

I suspected he'd been waiting decades to say this. I had an urge to tell him about myself as though I might be some next-generation consolation, tell him how I would like to be invited to his house and those big family get-togethers I'd always envied other people having, tell him I'd like him to meet my children, maybe read some of my stories where he could pick up a few things about my father. I would have liked to tell him that my father's history was fully sealed off from everyone. And about this most personal rejection? Well, he shouldn't take it personally.

I could see the curve of the Charles River from the apartment's ninth-floor window and watched as all those possible connections for my father—and me—were swept away on the spring current. My father had missed, by choice, I was learning, the opportunity for a wider embrace in the world, families who might have raised him, families, I learned later from some of his notes, that had tried and failed to make this happen.

I felt a surge of affection for this new relative of mine whom I would meet only once, weeks later, when he attended my father's memorial service. When he died not long after, before I had managed to visit him, I was surprised to feel such a new wave of mourning for how my father closed himself off from people who might have loved him.

But there was always his brother Howard, and every Sunday evening, when the long-distance rates went down, my father spoke to him on the phone. The conversations took place in his study with the door closed, and it would have been as unthinkable to interrupt him then as it would be to interrupt him while he was working. When the call was over and he came back into the kitchen, I tried to get a sense of what these brothers might have discussed, but he gave no clues or indication, no sign of a mood or shift. Even when those conversations must have been particularly difficult when Howard became terminally ill, the talks, each one possibly the last, were closed to me. But as Howard grew sicker, and my father sealed himself away for longer periods of time, his distress became harder to hide. One evening, right after one of these calls, he grabbed the handle of a pot simmering on the stove without a mitt, and in the instant it took for the pain to reach him, and then as he stood with his hand under cold water, still silent, I saw in him a kind of helpless grief I'd never seen before.

I barely knew Howard, his wife, or my two first cousins and remember only a few times we were ever together as families. Mamaroneck, New York, where they lived, was not so far away from Cambridge that we couldn't have seen them more often, but there were no holidays spent together and no regular visits, as other families seemed to do. As a kid, I had run on their perfect front lawn and had traced my finger down their raised wallpaper in a hallway. These atoms of impressions for years constituted my full picture of their life in Westchester County and were evidence of how different that existence was from ours in Cambridge; it was a distinction my parents touted. The material and psychic trappings of conventionality and suburban life that Howard, a lawyer in a prestigious New York firm, had fallen prey to appeared to be reason enough to mostly relegate the relationship between brothers to the confines of that Sunday phone call.

But I've always known this wasn't the whole story. After all, Howard, nine years older, had been my father's closest companion, his protector, his legal guardian soon after their father died. Details of the life of these boys were crumbs on the floor that I swept up after everyone else had left the room: they wandered the city, observed Hudson River whitefish (used condoms) floating by on the current, traveled to Europe, did their school work and washed behind their ears. They dropped pennies from the apartment window to see what would happen.

The brothers set out on their paths, and Howard had chosen the straighter course so my father could travel his wayward one for as long as he needed to, so that his life of creative exploration might fulfill the ultimate expression of their immigrant, book-reading, shirt-making, self-sacrificing father's desire for his youngest son. Howard, as with Twain and his brother Orion, was my father's "baseline for judging the distance he himself had traveled" from childhood, from the echoes of orphanhood. If my father's yard in Cambridge was a jungle with knee-high weeds, his house an eclectic mess of books and parties and acclaimed work, if he belonged to no synagogue and no country club, if he went to work without leaving the house, if his daughters swore freely and his wife went braless, this was made possible by Howard's decision to tend his garden in neat lines, to wear a suit and tie and paint his clapboards white.

"The younger brother had triumphed over the older brother in the same way that, in a certain sense he had triumphed over his father and his brother Henry . . . just by outliving them," my father wrote about Twain, perhaps presaging his own brother's early passing. This "triumph" came with a heavy burden of guilt Twain spent a lifetime attempting to numb, a dynamic that begins to explain my father's need to confine his relationship with his brother to the separate realm of his study.

One year in the early seventies, Howard and his family visited us briefly in Truro for an afternoon. The sweltering day and bleaching sun exposed everyone's uneasiness, and we moved in slow and deliberate motion. My father, barefoot and in his usual faded T-shirt and ragged shorts, smiled nervously as he set off on a epic marathon of scratching. He raked up and down his forearms, went at his neck with one hand and then the other. Tiny threads of blood ran down his sinewy calves. He was generally unaware of when he was scratching, and usually I barely noticed too because it was so habitual, but on this day, I couldn't look away. It hurt me to think how others might see him, wild with ectopic anguish, particularly his brother.

"Stop itching!" I told him.

It was an inside joke, shorthand for many things, including *I see your suffering* and *I'm sorry for it* and *You know you're only making it worse*. It was an affectionate command to stop doing something we all knew he couldn't stop, and a wink for using the word *itch* as both noun and verb, both cause and effect.

My father shrugged, but Howard's expression hardened as he came over to where I was sitting. I could barely look at him for how much he looked like my father. At eighteen, he had gotten sick with osteomyelitis in his leg, which had required multiple operations to address but never fully relieve the chronic pain he suffered from—without any self-pity, my father noted—and it had left him with a limp.

"You shouldn't say that," he said to me, banging his cane on the floor. "Your father has a disease. Would you make fun of someone with a disease? Of course not. And he is not itching; he is scratching."

My father smirked, perhaps recalling how in 1905, the Brooklyn Public Library in New York had banished *The Adventures of Huckleberry Finn* from the building's juvenile section for the same grammatical crime I'd apparently just committed: "Huck not only itched but scratched . . . said sweat when he should have said perspiration."

Still, Howard's scolding stung and caught me by surprise. My father knew there was nothing cruel about what I'd said—just the opposite—and I had not used the wrong word; I had misused it on purpose. I waited for him to defend me, but his allegiance was with his older brother. Until then, I had never thought of my father as someone with a disease; his skin was simply *him*. That Howard saw him another way was eye-opening, and a different portrait began to emerge as though I was already writing the story of him: my father, the boy plagued by eczema in a household of illness and a vigilant, mournful hush, a kid who still needed protection even as a man. My father had been bullied and beaten up at school as a child, scrawny, scratching, bookish, smart-ass, and mouthy, his glasses snatched and tossed. Howard had stood between him and anyone who dared add more misery to the mix, including now me.

Given the difference in their ages, their experience of their parents' deaths would not have been the same, but it was a shared and distinct bond. Their views of each other were historical, their former selves fully present during their phone calls, their current lives kept on the other side of closed doors. Together, there were too many other people in the room.

I was in college when Howard died in 1979, at the age of sixty-two. A rabbi led the service at the Frank E. Campbell Chapel on Madison Avenue. As we drove home later that afternoon, my parents poked fun at the pomp and stuffiness of the place, and the rabbi's generic praise of my uncle. It was clear that the man hadn't known Howard at all, but it was his calling Howard "a gentleman's gentleman"—a valet—that really got them howling, proof that the whole event was a sham.

"When his brother Henry died, [Twain] told Livy, he had not allowed himself to think of it, in case the grief should become too heavy," my father had written, as though already prepping himself for losing Howard. But laughing? The rabbi had made a harmless goof, and this is what they wanted to talk about? From the back seat, I was full of disapproval of their merciless mocking, their obvious aversion to sentiment. Even the loss of the person he was closest to, the one person who connected his present to his past, couldn't open my father to tears, not even here, in private in the car with his wife and three children, on the day of his only brother's funeral.

But this is just a fiction about what happened in the car that day; this is evidence of my aversion too, my falseness.

The real version is this, what the writer must finally tangle with if she is to arrive at any measure of truth: During

Howard's funeral service, I had made myself busy—observe, observe, observe, evade, evade, evade—by noting the backs of my cousins' frizzy heads and their pale necks above their too-big collars, my aunt dressed in black, Georgia trembling, her hat throwing shaky shadows across her shoulders, my father scribbling something on the service program with his gold pencil, the chapel's sueded gray light. I was pleased with my eye for detail. When the rabbi delivered his doomed line about the gentleman's gentleman, I knew that *this* was the story I was going to tell to make people smile and shake their heads and I could avoid having to talk or contend with anything painful—particularly loss. I had learned from my father how the deflection, the tease and the joke, relieve us from the implications of our own emotions, but also how they keep us apart from not only ourselves but those who might offer solace. "The secret source of humor itself is not joy but sorrow. There is no humor in heaven," Twain had said. I was not disapproving of my laughing father; I was just like him.

Many years after Howard's death, I asked my father why he didn't have any contact with Howard's two sons who, after all, had been left fatherless just as he had been. Without looking up from the counter where he was chopping onions, he said that the responsibility had felt too big. He knew he couldn't live up to their expectations of him to be another father, or even a hands-on uncle. He felt guilty about it, an unusual and tender admission. But he hadn't failed in trying, it seems to me now; he'd failed in his decision to not try at all. He had written about Twain's "oppressive sense of obligation" to his mother and siblings, as if sensing his own struggle between hoarding the private self and the giving freely of it, as terrifying as that is, between a need to face the pain and a greater need to shut it out.

Of all the writers who came to the house, the poet L. E. Sissman was rare and different, in part because he had what my parents called "a real job" as an advertising executive. To me, that meant that he put on work clothes and real shoes every day, maybe picked up a briefcase, and left for an office where he attended meetings, used a stapler and a three-hole punch, and poured himself a cup of coffee from the office pot. Because my father had an endless enthusiasm for office supplies, which we would buy him every year for his birthday—erasers, mechanical pencils, pads, date and time stampers, rubber thimbles, rubber bands, tape dispensers—I suspected that on some days he envied the security and routine of his friend's job.

Ed, as my parents called him, was tall and stooped, and he had a way of fluidly moving through the rooms, head and neck first, that reminded me of a giraffe. I never saw him without his pipe. He was reserved, more contained than the others who came to the house; he was not hungry for attention, for making the right connections, not at all on the take. He was like my father in some ways, calm and seemingly without ego, satisfied perhaps by having done a good day of work. He smiled at me in the same warm but distant way. My father treated him with great affection and attentiveness, and a kind of solicitousness I'd never seen before from him and didn't understand.

I would have asked Ed a million questions if I could have about what it was like to be a poet. Why was he so quiet among these other writers and without their anxious, competitive energy? I would have told him that I knew exactly where his books were shelved in the living room among the many volumes of poetry, that I'd read them but doubted my own understanding. *Dying: An Introduction* had a vaguely cartoonish drawing of a blue gravestone; the letters of the title looked carved in granite. I would have told him that the lighthearted sketch and the downhearted title confused me.

A few days after one of the parties, the oversensitive plumbing in the house began to revolt and the toilet in the bathroom on the first floor backed up. An eggy stink climbed the stairs and into our bedrooms. I came home from school to see a crew of men leaning on shovels and looking into an enormous hole in what had been the front yard. They had found the problem: Ed's pipe was lodged in a pipe.

"Ceci n'est pas une pipe," my father said, dreamily.

Later, he said that Ed had told him the morning after the party that he'd accidentally dropped his pipe into the toilet, flushed without thinking, and watched it disappear. There had been a guest the year before who'd peed in the grandfather clock, and maybe Ed had also drunk too much. Or maybe he'd opened his mouth to try out a line of poetry in his head. Maybe he'd laughed at the sound of his own wild words—*electrotypers, gumballs, bird-wife, unfingermarked, stertorous radamacues.*

My father said he didn't have the heart to tell Ed about what his flushed pipe had done. The damage and the cost were enormous, but there was beauty in the episode for my father, and I could tell that it had come to occupy that warmly lit place we revisit to feel again our own awe at moments of communion, the kind of moment I would attempt to capture in my writing. "Elegy deepened, as his long-foreseen death reared, to anguish," Updike wrote about Sissman's late work in a review of his collected poems, perhaps remembering how they'd more than once stood together at our back door looking at the linden tree. And I'd stood watching them, envious of something I couldn't yet name. Already a seasoned companion on the final journeys of others, my father never told me that Ed was sick by that time and that a diagnosis of Hodgkin's lymphoma had by then traveled with him for years. He didn't tell me how death is not separate from living, as he knew all too well. There was nowhere in the house to acknowledge or attend to this. There was no talk of death or how it might give meaning to life. My father left that for his book; it's all there on every page. Ed died at forty-eight.

Twain, upon the death of his brother Orion, had written, "He was good—all good and sound; there was nothing bad in him, nothing base, nor any unkindness." Forty years after Howard's funeral, I found a crumbling copy of the eulogy my father had delivered, tucked into that service program he'd scribbled on with his gold pencil. That I hadn't remembered he'd stood before the mourners in the chapel and spoke so deeply and powerfully is evidence of how I was barely present for the reality and sorrow of the day.

For me he was not only an older brother, teacher, companion, and, despite the difference in our ages, playmate: he was also, in every sense of the word, a guardian, fiercely protective . . . I am the beneficiary of his patience, tolerance, and kindness . . . I think Howard believed that the best course in pilgrimages was not to concern oneself with theology or liturgy or the like but instead to take short views, hope for the best, trust in God, and try to get to your goal . . . One of his guidelines must have been "Whatsoever thy hand intended to do, do with all thy might; for there is no work, nor device, nor knowledge, nor wisdom, in the grave."

Like Howard I do not pretend to know about long-terms effects. But it is impossible for me not to believe that Howard's goodness and love survive him . . . [and] become a part of us. And so there may be some reason for giving thanks.

Whole lines have faded, but I feel his words today, rendered sacred by the manner in which they were written and trembling with truth on the page.

Twelve

Cuckoo Clocks

•

"When he built his own house there, that eccentric, willful, and eye-catching whatnot, $70,000 worth of turrets and balconies housing $21,000 worth of furniture and perched on a five-acre $31,000 tract of land, Nook Farm received from its newest member its gaudiest landmark, and eventually, instead of merely going into debt, Clemens went into bankruptcy."

In the longest winter of writing this book, I was eager to leave the present and trace the steps of my daydreams for a morning, so I drove to the Mark Twain House in Hartford. I had been there last more than fifty years earlier when my father, a few years after the publication of his book, had been invited for a private tour with his family. The vastness of the visitor center, new since I was nine years old, suggested that were it not for a pandemic the place would be packed with school kids waiting to walk through the home of America's Most Famous Writer. But today, midweek, it was almost empty except for the few masked people waiting for the tour to start. I bristled at their presence. This was *my* house, after all, in a way it could never be for them.

We followed the tour guide past the closed Nook Farm Café toward the house. The city had grown up and around the house and the neighborhood, once known as Nook Farm, home to Harriet Beecher Stowe and other influential thinkers and scholars. On Farmington Avenue, just beyond, there was a pizza place, a laundromat, and a convenience store in a low-slung strip of businesses that had seen better days. The guide stopped to give the group some basic information about the history and dazzling scale of the 11,500-square-foot place we were about to enter. "The conspicuous symbol of [Twain's] success as a writer . . . the Word was made bricks and mortar," my father had written. I had his book with me, and as I read, it was as though through his precise description, the structure took form in front of me for the first time.

> Outside and inside it defied all categories. It presented to the dazzled eye three turrets, the tallest of which was octagonal and about fifty feet high, five balconies, innumerable embrasures, a huge shaded veranda that turned a corner, an elaborate porte-cochere, a forest of chimneys. Its dark brick walls were trimmed with brownstone and decorated with inlaid designs in scarlet-painted brick and black; the roof was patterned in colored tile. The house was permanent polychrome and gingerbread Gothic; it was part steamboat, part medieval stronghold, and part cuckoo clock.

The guide ushered us into the chilly entrance hall and told us that the light inside the house was dim to reflect what it would have been like when Twain lived there, and that it might take a moment for our eyes to adjust after the brightness outside. For a few seconds, it was like stepping into a fog, visual and temporal, and when I gazed up the stairwell to the very highest point of the house, the view framed by the ornate woodwork and balustrades and dizzied by silver stenciled patterns everywhere, I shivered with the sensation of having been there before.

Back then, my nine-year-old self had conjured the bodily warmth of Twain's three daughters, my other sisters, when they passed close by me in the entrance hall. I had heard the rustling of their dresses, noticed the scuff on their shoes, listened to their chatter, smelled dried roses and soap. I had seen Twain too in that first visit, descending the stairs, and glimpsed his wife Livy, frail and white, in the conservatory. I had been living with this family for so many years that for a moment we lived again under the same fanciful roof.

But on this visit half a century later, Twain and his family didn't return to me, perhaps having been thoroughly stilled by these years of reading and thinking and writing about them so much. Instead, it was my father in a tweed jacket and tie I saw walking through the rooms again. I saw my mother and my sisters in dresses and reflected pride trailing him. He was lit up, happy, feeling good about himself, soaking in the pleasures of respect this private tour by the museum's director signaled. My father stopped to look at the fireplace, the flue diverted to either side of it to accommodate the window above the mantelpiece because Twain liked "watching snow-flakes and flames at the same time." He remembered how Twain had "installed some tin roofing over the house because he liked to hear the rain drumming," and for a moment I saw him returned to another man's sensory contemplations and contentments. Perhaps he had returned to mine too, and my childhood habit of leaving every window open so I could hear all kinds of weather.

"Inside, on three stories, were nineteen large rooms, five baths (with indoor plumbing, which was still a novelty," my father had written, "and washbasins decorated to harmonize with the rugs), and a wealth of idiosyncratic delights . . . The furnishings were heavy, ornate, and, like the mantel-pieces, opulently inlaid and carved with cherubs, gargoyles, sphinxes, and griffins."

Every night, the guide explained, Twain would tell his children a new story, always starting with the painting of a cat in a ruff—a fanciful fluted collar that looked like a cup-cake holder—and using the objects and art on the shelf that ran above the fireplace. I was distantly disappointed by the familiarity of the cat painting, as though I'd gone to Ver-sailles and discovered in a bedroom the same lamp I'd bought at IKEA. We all nodded in appreciation of Twain's feat of de-voted parenting, but I saw on my conjured father's face some skepticism at this spin of familial harmony. Children! My fa-ther knew what they did to your work, your concentration, your freedom.

I saw that my evoked father detected, as I did, the smell of dying flowers coming from the elegant semicircular conservatory attached to the library, where winter could be converted into summer and nature could be moved indoors, with white pebble paths, plants, bubbling fountain, and humidity. Something needed to be cleaned, unclogged. Houses like this eat people; maybe the place was short on money. As the tour made its way through the rest of the house, the playroom, the girls' room, the nursery, the bedrooms and bathrooms, the school room that had been Twain's study until he'd ceded it to his children, the anodyne vibe turned decidedly and devotedly domestic.

Here was the small chair next to the big chair where one of Twain's children sat as he read to her. I saw irritation on my father's face as we were invited to imagine the serene father-daughter scene. He had written that "'How [Twain] would be affected by this or that no one could ever foresee,' Clara wrote after his death. She still remembered that as children she and her sisters were often terrified of being left alone with him. He was charming and entertaining with them, told endless stories and invented games and romps, but his mood might shift without warning from light to dark, his brow suddenly cloud over, and he would speak to them in anger or with autocratic severity." He knew that the real story was always more complicated. But still, with ghosts sitting in the big and little chairs, who could resist returning for an instant to their own childhood bathed in moments of sunlight, his father reading Jules Verne to him, my father reading Poe's "The Cask of Amontillado" to me.

Here's where Twain and his wife slept, the tour guide pointed out, their heads at the foot of the bed so they could see the angels carved into the headboard; here's where they ate their family meals and served guests "claret and champagne, filet of beef and canvasback ducks, Nesselrode pudding and ice cream angels." On the third floor was the billiard room, ornate, rich, full of good fortune and light, which had also been Twain's study. When I'd first visited, the room hadn't been open to the public, but it had been for us on that special day, and with the museum director standing nearby, I'd been aware then of getting a glimpse of something maybe too private to be seen. Now there was an admission of that breach in the staged scattering of pages on the billiard's felt, pool cues and balls at interrupted angles as though the game and the work happened at the same time. This was why the schoolkids were marched here year after year: to see the genius at work so the secret of success could be revealed.

And there was my imagined father in the room again, leaning toward his own conjured Twain who was scribbling something on one of those pages. I could tell by how he scratched his cheek and ineffectively cleared his throat, how much he longed to caution the man to be wiser with his money, his schemes, and his investments, his fame, his psyche, to not let his daughters out of his sight, to prepare because the storms of loneliness and guilt were coming. But as the biographer, my father had to hold knowledge and ignorance, past, present, and future, flash back and flash forward at the same time, keep his mouth shut, and allow the story to unfold. As do I to keep myself from telling my father that if he remained so hidden, his children would end up feeling they'd never known him, that he'd never known them, that this would bloom as unshakable sadness in their middle age. That I would end up writing this book about him, hoping to change the course of things.

The tour guide moved us into the wide hall, and as the light shifted from outside as if on cue, I knew exactly what was coming. I knew how this story ended, and I wanted all of us to leave before we had to hear it. My finger was already on the page where my father had written: "The domestic idyll, played out in the great house in Hartford filled with children and visitors . . . ended in drawn out grief. His favorite daughter (and clearest eyed biographer), Susy, died in 1896."

The family never returned to live in the house, and it was eventually sold. "Susy spent her last two weeks back in her own house, walked the floor in pain and delirium, became blind, and died after being in a coma for two days," my father had described. "What [Twain] desperately searched for was some sign that before she died she had him in her thoughts, spoke of him in pride or love . . . 'When out of her head,' he wrote in his notebook, 'she said many things that showed she was proud of being my daughter.'"

I saw my father standing with Twain by the stairwell, hand on the banister. He couldn't make the world whole again for Twain; he couldn't end the man's desperate search. He could only be present for it. "After a lifetime of hunting for a crime which he could say he had committed, [Twain's] guilt had finally crystallized so massively around this real event that his grief at Livy's death eight years later hardly compared in intensity. Their loss, he now said, 'would bankrupt the vocabularies of all the languages to put into words,' and, in another image central to his experience, he said that Susy's death was like a man's house burning down—it would take him years and years to discover all that he had lost in the fire."

My father's vocabulary was bankrupt when it came to talking about all he had lost in the fire, but he had written about how obeisance to the rituals of mourning made him "weep for my imprisoned self, my neck in its collar, my toes in their shoes, and for all the glories of the bright day outside." His unspoken grief is the fuel that reminds him he is in fact very much still alive and reminds me that is it not mine finally to take on anymore.

My father had built another house after his own family's fire, one that was vibrant and full of fortune and purpose, and now as he stands with Twain, he recalls a time when his teenage daughters had asked for their own house keys, but he'd said no as though the house didn't also belong to them, as though they were guests. It hadn't ended well for him and they'd screamed and insulted him. He'd had three new keys made the next day, which he'd wrapped in tissue paper and ribbons so they might understand that his past was not theirs.

I left my father and Twain outside the billiard room and followed the tour group being ushered down the back staircase like overstaying guests. I bought some postcards from the gift shop where I spotted other copies of my father's book, published over fifty years earlier, on the shelf among all the many, many other books about Twain. There were Mark Twain key rings, and notepads and dish towels, mugs that said, *Writing is easy. All you have to do is cross out the wrong words* and *The world owes you nothing. It was here first.* On the drive home, I remembered where I'd seen that painting of the cat in a ruff before: it was framed and hung in my parents' bathroom at one time, just to the right of the window that looked out into the trees and the snowstorms and the rain.

I wanted to see another house from the past I shared with my father, and the day after I went to Hartford, I drove to Cambridge. My parents had sold the place on Francis Avenue years before to what one of the remaining neighbors had called with tenacious academic disdain an "entrepreneur." No one other than a multimillionaire could afford to live on Professors Row these days. Renovations that had begun soon after the sale—gone were the lilac bushes, the porch with the Ping-Pong table, even the front steps, though the fluted columns remained—appeared permanently stalled, and the house sat with half of it clad in Tyvek, its upstairs windows covered in plywood. At first glance, you could imagine there'd been a fire inside. I considered peeking through the window of my father's study but decided I didn't want to see what it looked like now.

Already half a century old when my parents had bought it in 1959, the house had needed constant tending, but my parents mostly let it fend for itself. It sighed through its aging and aches; it was too expensive to keep warm, to keep clean, to make fully healthy ever again. If evidence of a slow leak crept down a wall, blossoming the paint and forcing the horsehair plaster to fissure and fall, it was just easiest to shut the door to the room and never open it again. When the leaded glass

windows that flanked the front door cracked, a piece of Plexi-
glas was installed behind them, sealing in the damage, the
dead bugs, and permanent water drops.

When Twain's house in Hartford had "devoured their
energies and their money," Twain had "felt that what the
house needed most of all was an incendiary to put them out
of their misery." The floor of my childhood bedroom had
been bright turquoise linoleum, not wood as in the rest of the
house, the result of one of the previous owner's kids playing
with matches and almost burning the place down. That a fire
had happened right where I slept occurred to me every night,
stoking my taste for high tragedy.

Still standing in front of the house, I remembered one afternoon in the carpool on our way home from school when
we'd come to a line of fire engines at the far end of a street
where the boy in the back seat lived. Wouldn't it be funny
if it was your house, we all joked, until we saw a burning
couch being dragged out of his front door. I was afraid to turn
around and see on his face what it looked like when you understood that your home and your life had forever changed.

Since I'd first visited Twain's house as a child, I had returned to it in my mind as often as I still return to the one
on Francis Avenue. The houses are one and the same. Here
are the cats and the plants both men tended. Here is the wallpaper each man saw upon waking. Here is the window that
let in the moonlight that woke them but they didn't mind, so
enchanted to see the orb beyond the glass. Here is the body
next to theirs, a comfort against the fears of the night. Here
are the children still asleep, here are the children leaving

home because it's time. Here is the desk, the paper, the pen and pencil. When you close your eyes, everyone is still alive and emerging from their rooms, and you accept that they will be different people today than they were yesterday, and what you hold on to is the smile they offer and the questions they put to you, and the way they throw on a jacket and invite you to go on a walk with them by the river. Already I see that when I leave the house I live in, it will join those other two.

In my parents' last year in the house on Francis Avenue, a raccoon, or more than one, had started coming in through the dog door and tearing the kitchen apart at night. Crackers, nuts, and tipped glasses were everywhere, the floor sticky with dirty paw prints. An unripe avocado had been nibbled, a martini olive was under the table. The cats had begun to bring in birds too, which they toyed with before killing under my parents' bed. My parents were not dismayed then or ever. They did not nail the dog door shut or keep the cats inside. For them this anarchy was exciting, but it also must have been a sign, like the bloody wing prints left on their ceiling by the damaged and doomed birds, that it was time to leave.

Thirteen

How to Read and Write

•

"Sentence by sentence and paragraph by paragraph, Mark Twain was an entirely deliberate and conscious craftsman; he insisted that the difference between the nearly right word and the right word was the difference between the lightning bug and the lightning; his ear for the rhythms of speech was unsurpassed, and he demanded in dialect and social notation nothing short of perfection. But his larger and structural methods were inspirational and intuitive."

When the movie *Love Story* came out in 1970, my father and I went to see it one January afternoon at the Fresh Pond Cinema. We had watched parts of it being filmed in Harvard Yard, and many of the locations were thrillingly familiar to me; Oxford Street, where the doomed lovers lived, was just around the corner from our house. Every seat in the theater was filled, and I was attuned to the humid, weepy air and the growing distress of the audience over the fate of Jenny and

Oliver. Next to me, my father ate popcorn and giggled. When it was over, people stayed in their seats to dab their eyes and collect themselves before the lights came fully on, while my father and I marched up the aisle before anyone else, smug and coolly unmoved by what we'd just seen.

My pose of imperviousness to the movie's high drama clearly meant I had powers of discernment and taste, like my father, and unlike the rest of the audience. It meant I could recognize schlock in an instant and would be immune to manipulation when Jenny, tear-streaked, red-nosed, and shivering on her sagging front steps, says to Oliver, "Love means never having to say you're sorry."

"Really, is that not one of the dumbest lines ever written?" my father asked, when we stepped out into the gray afternoon.

(Years later, as general editor of *Bartlett's Familiar Quotations*, my father, recognizing the line's cultural weight, included it in the latest edition, to sit among such greats as "It ain't over till it's over" (Yogi Berra) and "At bottom God is nothing other than an exalted father" (Sigmund Freud) and "To love, cherish, and to obey" (The Book of Common Prayer). When Terry Gross of *Fresh Air* asked him about the inclusion of the *Love Story* line, my father said, "It's so stupid and so meaningless that again it became burned in the American memory.")

As we drove home from the movie, we wondered if the line even made sense. Didn't love, in fact, mean you *had* to say you were sorry? In our family, apology had oversize importance—by offering it, all was set right again supposedly—but with little lasting meaning. My father and I talked about the irony of Oliver's icy WASP father who arrives too late to be of any use to anyone, blinking under the awning that reads MT. SINAI HOSPITAL AND KLINGEN-STEIN PAVILION. I was always on the lookout for a Jewish name, and here were two in an unlikely moment. The cultural clues were leaden, we agreed, or were they just careless? (At eleven, what could I have possibly understood about this?)

We laughed over Jenny's impassioned speech in the hospital—"Screw Paris, screw music and all those things you think you stole from me"—but I was eager to hear, what *did* a person say on her deathbed? I had imagined that my father actually knew the answer to this, twice over. It had begun to sleet, and the wipers slapped to keep up. Tell me, I thought, and I'll never ask you again. Don't ask, don't ask, don't ask, the wipers warned. I thought he would shatter if I asked, so I didn't. The physical sensation of being unable to ask him those questions is still with me, my own esprit d'escalier, and when I began to write fiction, this feeling of having missed my chance was a reminder to me to make my characters do and say all those things I wasn't brave enough to do or say myself.

Later that summer, months after we'd seen the movie, I met—as much as a child can meet any adult—Erich Segal, author of *Love Story*, at a cocktail party at the Wellfleet summer home of a Harvard professor. My sisters and I had been unhappily dragged along by my parents, and my presence was so fully inconsequential that I see myself as someone other than me in order to see myself there at all: a goofy-looking girl in glasses, in boy's jean cutoffs and a Dennis the Menace–style striped T-shirt. Insecurity is written all over me and the way I cross my arms over my chest and won't make eye contact. What was I doing there inside, the only child, when my sisters were waiting outside? Everyone in the room was successful, it seemed to me, their names preceded by *best-selling author, artist, architect, actor, award-winning journalist.* The air shimmered with self-importance. That summer, I'd been occupied by a pernicious and worrisome question: If you died unknown, did that mean you'd led a meaningless life? It was starting to seem more and more likely that this was true—and would be true for me.

I watched Segal, the guest-of-honor writer whose posture was receptive to the guests' attention, almost liquid in his comfort, one elbow propped on a bookcase. Out the window, I saw my sisters sitting on a low wall next to where the dusty old cars were haphazardly parked. There would be a dented bumper or sideswipe before the evening was over; everyone would have had too much to drink, and they would wave away the dings and dents, attesting to how little they cared about material things. My sisters didn't share my need to be close to the action. I envied what looked like their ease and their lack of preoccupation with themselves, and at the same time hoped some of the noise and light of the party might enter my bloodstream. I was a young masochist, too easily swayed by my mother's assurances that this kind of thing was good for me if I was going to be a writer. (But I never said I wanted to be a writer, I told her.) My parents were at their very charming social best with the guest of honor—warm, enthusiastic, jokey—my mother in the same long linen dress half the other women were wearing too, topped off with an enameled peace sign on a leather string, my father in a collared shirt and bare feet. Segal said something and my father looked down, noting the melting ice in his glass, ready to leave. He didn't like being there any more than I did, while my mother laughed, showing the room the underside of her chin.

When I looked again at the writer, I heard the echo of my father saying, *Really, is that not one of the dumbest lines ever written?*

After the party, the drive took us back through the dimming, single-file dirt roads of the exclusive and private Wellfleet woods. Hand-painted signs at each fork, illuminated by the headlights, announced familiar names and false dead ends, a ploy to keep outsiders out. As my father put the car into reverse to let another car pass, he swore, flustered and swatting at mosquitoes. He hadn't wanted to go to that fucking party in the first place, with all its smug and self-satisfied guests and its airlessness. What would have been wrong with staying home, having a drink, watching the sun set, and reading a book? My mother, still high from the party fumes, twisted the cord of her necklace.

In his distress, my father had somehow taken a wrong turn, and now we were lost, the silky kettle ponds barely glinting between the scrub pines at that hour. My sisters and I hung over the front seat, collecting our weapons of ridicule, but we knew not to say a word at that moment. Getting lost was a fear of my father's that spoke to failure, to urgency, and maybe to never being found. (I thought at that moment about the writer who had lived in these woods and died in his house alone. When he was finally found, it was discovered that his dogs, crazed with hunger after weeks, had been nibbling at his corpse.)

The road's shoulders were dangerously fragile, and sand pinged the car as the tires spun. "If your car was stuck in the soft sand, you were not likely to be rescued (except, in extremity, by the Mobil station's tow truck)," my father wrote about these Wellfleet woods in an article for *Harper's Magazine* in 2011. "Seeing you trying to dig your car out of a treacherous shoulder after it had spun its wheels and sunk even deeper, residents in a passing car might slow down just long enough to remind you to put the sand back where you found it."

Finally, out of the woods, and out again on Route 6, the mood in the car relaxed and my parents began the party's postmortem. Writers who made it big by writing what my parents called junk (sometimes synonymous with best-sellers) were obvious targets and Segal was not an exception. He had taught classics at Yale at one point, but now apparently his bellbottom white pants were their own kind of downwind pretension. And all those starstruck guests and their fawning. And what a dopey book! But I was confused. Look how well Segal had done, money, a movie, lots of attention. Was this maybe just envy? When they talked about others, how could my parents remove themselves from the crowd if they were also part of it?

When we stopped at a light, I saw people, some still in bathing suits with soggy towels at their waists, waiting to buy fried clams and soft serve at PJ's. Their pleasures seemed uncomplicated, their only goals divided under the neon-lit awnings into sweet or salty. The world was full of the extraordinary and the ordinary—though which was which that night, I wasn't sure then and still am not today—and the passage between the two appeared as mazelike as those roads in the woods and as dangerous as Route 6 with its sun-addled drivers.

On the evening after we'd gone to see *Love Story*, as my sisters and I ate dinner and my parents had their cocktails, my father disappeared into his study and returned with a book to read to us, as he often did.

"Listen to this," he said.

If he noticed our eyes rolling, he ignored it. Like Twain, he "read poetry aloud to the ladies." (Like Twain, he was also "a writer surrounded by women and seeking their approval.") My mother shushed us, though we were already silent, the kitchen stage prepared for him. He cleared his throat, blushed, never comfortable being the center of attention, even at home, even with just us.

From all the rest I single out you, having a message
    for you:
You are to die—Let others tell you what they please,
    I cannot
prevaricate,
I am exact and merciless, but I love you—There is
    no escape for

you. Softly I lay my right hand upon you—you just
    feel it,
I do not argue—I bend my head close, and half
    envelope it,
I sit quietly by—I remain faithful,
I am more than nurse, more than parent or neighbor,
I absolve you from all except yourself, spiritual,
    bodily—that is
eternal—
You yourself will surely escape,
The corpse you will leave will be but
    excrementitious.
The sun bursts through in unlooked-for directions!
Strong thoughts fill you, and confidence—you smile!
You forget you are sick, as I forget you are sick,
You do not see the medicines—you do not mind the
    weeping
friends—I am with you,
I exclude others from you—there is nothing to be
    commiserated,
I do not commiserate—I congratulate you.

What spurred him to read Whitman's "To One Shortly
to Die" on this particular night he didn't say, but Whitman
was always on his mind those days, even as he was working on a new biography of Lincoln Steffens. (Whitman and I
share a birthday. We could have blown out the candles on the
cake together.) He lived and breathed Whitman and the "un-
lovely city of Camden," *Leaves of Grass*, burial grounds, and

daguerreotypes. For now, though, in the kitchen, my father looked transported by what he'd just read to us and hopeful that we might find it as extraordinary as he did. His eyes were bright, but he'd missed the mark. Whitman wasn't *our* world, and poetry was not our language, and we were silent. My sisters had more patience than I did for the awkward moment and less interest in stemming the disappointment creeping over his face. Susanna reached for the sports section of the paper. Polly fed the dog under the table, and I rushed in to ease my father's hurt.

"What does *excrementitious* mean?" I asked, already pretty sure I knew what it meant.

"Look it up," my father said, dejected. (The dictionary, of which there were many within easy reach throughout the house, was a sacred book, and looking up a word was a sacred act accompanied by the suggestion that we might even learn something in the process.) He went back to his study, where I imagined he returned the book to his desk and gave it a commiserating pat.

"You girls are terrible," my mother said. "So mean."

I guiltily cleared my plate. I knew that my father was showing us—maybe even showing me alone—something important about writing: what was good and what wasn't, what was real and what was recycled hot air, but I couldn't make sense of it. He'd been touched by Whitman's words but not *Love Story*'s? What was the difference between him moved in the kitchen and those weepers in the movie theater who had been moved too by the bedside scene? What was the difference between what he'd read us and what they'd heard? My father was showing us that the real culprit was writing that took itself too seriously, claimed unearned gravitas and peddled wholesale shams and "pretentious falsities." But how was one to tell the truth of experience from the lie if the truth was never talked about? My father could have told us what witnessing the end was like, put it in his own words instead of Whitman's, or even Segal's, but he didn't.

Later in bed, the sleet having turned to heavy snow and the likelihood of a day off from school, I fought the urge to *feel* what the movie had tempted me with: "Would you do something for me?" Jenny had asked Oliver with her last breath. "Would you please hold me?" Ryan O'Neal was very handsome; it wouldn't be terrible to be held by him.

The sun bursts through in unlooked-for directions! Strong thoughts fill you, and confidence—you smile!

What would it have been like to have given in to weepiness in the theater or even then in my room alone, dampening my pillow where no one could see, and shed an increasingly suffocating self-consciousness that was my own sham, my own pretentious falsity? To be moved openly by the peddled sentiment seemed dangerous, a gateway drug to ordinariness. I wanted to give in, but I didn't, and I still don't, although today, deep into writing this story of my father, I feel myself finally inching toward an understanding that it wasn't ordinariness I feared, but a depth of feeling I thought might swallow me up.

Maybe for my father, this public hardening—if I see it as a calcification of the heart today, I can be softer with him— had always been a matter of survival. I see him at thirteen in Riverside Park during the mourning period for his father. The Hudson River is in front of him, the city at his back, no mother or father at home anymore to open the door for him when he returns, to call hello from the other room, to use a finger to wipe a crumb from his chin. The sap of mourning rises in him. His fingers twitch, and a fluttering fills his chest. How long will he be alone? He knows he might drown if he takes his eyes off the boat going north, if he feels anything more than pure wonder at the way its prow parts the water.

As a child, my father kept lists of newly discovered words and their definitions in private notebooks. He must have sensed their value already, even if he didn't know what he would do with them. One day he'd uttered the word *hell* in seventh grade just to see what power it might have: it got him sent home. He didn't see anything wrong with the much-maligned opening, "It was a dark and stormy night." After all, he claimed, it said exactly what it meant.

He was thrilled by a good malapropism and appreciated the beauty of a mangled sentence, but the real assault was sloppiness and imprecision. In his short and uneasy stint teaching in an MFA creative writing program in his seventies, his earlier teaching days at Harvard forgotten, he had called to tell me about a student's misspelling of *T-shirt* (or is it *tee-shirt* or *tee shirt?*) He bounced between disbelief and dismay, a reaction so overblown that I laughed and said not every writer was as fastidious as he was. After all, I asked, did it really matter that much?

"Getting it right is the *only* thing that matters," he said.

"In writing about Mark Twain, you are going to writing school with a very great writer. You're constantly learning prose from a master. You wish you could do it over again, better," he told an interviewer. Still, he was not above calling out Twain when he fell short: "The contrasts he used" to describe the ruins of Baalbek, "came too glibly, a mechanical formula for disposing of the past: the blocks were as big as omnibuses or freight cars or streetcars, with none smaller than a carpenter's chest and some larger than the hull of a steamboat." I read his prose as carefully as he reads Twain's, and I am struck by Joe's use of *disposing*, instead of *considering* or even *viewing*, a word that suggests a too-efficient finality.

As an adult, he still kept lists of words and phrases, thrilled by those he didn't know, or whose sounds delighted his ears:

> *Strange attractor*
> *The Great Rann of Kutch*
> *Bluefin—horse mackerel—tuna—thunfish—tunny—*
>   *thunnus*
> *Scombroid*
> *Salp*
> *Tomography—X-ray plane sections*
> *Copula*
> *Scruff*
> *Scumble*
> *Coppice*
> *Gallybagger*
> *Collop*

Sternutatory

Favonian

Hebephrenia

Imbricated

Peplus, etc.

Walking the dog by the Harvard Divinity School one afternoon, he asked me if I knew the difference between *coprophage* and *coprophilia*. Take the words apart, he'd instructed. Words were puzzles and treasure chests, capable of making you feel and see. He adored the languages of lives unfamiliar to him; acronyms and expressions of the US Marine Corps, the police, evangelical preachers, small-time bureaucrats, wise-guys, butchers, car repairmen, New Age practitioners, stuffy academics. A medical lexicon was a feast: *axillary*; *exsanguinate*; *popliteal*, *Wenckebach*, *vestibular*, *coccyx*, *atresia*. He thumbed through the *Merck Manual* for the names of rare afflictions that he would rattle off when we played Ping-Pong.

In New York one day when I was in college, he and I had stopped to look at the Empire State Building. *Skyscraper* was the first word he fell in love with, he told me in a rare moment of nostalgia, because it was a word that once seen cannot be unseen. The object was animated when it was coupled with intent; *scraper* suggests striving and aspiration, maybe something that's just brushed by your fingertips. "[Twain] was fond of simple mechanistic images," he had written. "('Waiting for the tanks to fill up again,' he would say during a 'dry' spell)" or the image in *The Innocents Abroad* of the Milanese barber's razor that regained its sharp edge after resting for a while on the shelf. "It was a way," my father wrote, "of writing about the sources of creative energy." I am fond of this particular mechanistic image when it comes to my father: a skyscraper reaching into the clouds, my father reaching to grab a bit of it, his hand coming away full of air, but his head full of words. I told him the first word I fell in love with was *sweetheart*, half cannibal, half candy.

Familiar himself with writing's obstacles, he described how Twain approached certain blocks "in the same way that the tongue comes back to the site of the missing tooth." He was clear about what it took to write well: you wrote, then rewrote, and rewrote again until you got it right.

At fifteen, I got up the nerve to show my father a paper I had written for school and was due the following day. Sitting over the heating vent in my room, I'd worked harder on the essay about *Gideon's Trumpet* by Anthony Lewis than I'd ever worked on anything. The fact that Lewis had been to our house a few times gave me the misguided idea that my observations might be unusually incisive.

I'd delivered the paper to Joe's study after dinner and retreated to my room while he read it. It is agony waiting while your work is being read—that particular torture never goes away—I knew there were weaknesses and holes in my argument, but I thought I could get away with them. I'd worked so hard, and for so long; the effort alone had to be worth something. I should have known better, having witnessed my father read my mother's work. With his gold pencil, he went line by line. His markings spun around single words, sentences, around phrases, around the space between ideas and scenes. Nothing escaped scrutiny.

Finally, my father called me into his study. He'd taken his pencil to my paper, and the margins were filled with squiggly lines, wiry question marks, words I couldn't decipher. I felt chilled and panicky. Be specific, concrete, he kept saying. What does this sentence mean? Is this the best word, the right word? I struggled to stay focused.

"So, this is a start," he said, handing the pages back to me. "Now you need to write it a few more times until you figure out what it is you're trying to say."

I told him that his standards were ridiculous, that he was wrong, that the paper was good enough the way it was, and besides, it was due the next morning, but he had no sympathy for my dismay. Polly recalls the torture of having him type up a school paper for her but making her edit it as he did, calling out each sentence, asking over and over for clarity, his disappointment clear. He was wounded by our sloppiness and what he must have thought was our indifference but more confused by why we would be angry at him, when he was only trying to help, when he was only applying the same standards he applied to his own work.

My father was incapable of modulating how he read anyone else's work, even his children's. For him, it was honesty or nothing at all, and his critique of a piece of writing could be harsh and exacting, and not everyone had the stomach for it. He would often say no to reading the manuscript of a friend or colleague not because he was ungenerous with his time and attention, but because he understood the immense responsibility of the undertaking if he was going to do it right and how everything was riding on it for the writer.

My father gives considerable attention to Twain's 1876 story, "The Facts Concerning the Recent Carnival of Crime in Connecticut," and must have felt some uneasy identification with it when the narrator's conscience, embodied by a vile little creature, pokes at the narrator for saying no to reading a young woman's work.

In the story, the narrator explains, "I told that girl, in the kindest, gentlest way, that I could not consent to deliver judgment upon any one's manuscript, because an individual's verdict was worthless."

To which his conscience retorts: "Yes, you said all that. So you did, you juggling, small-souled shuffler! And yet when the happy hopefulness faded out of that poor girl's face, when you saw her furtively slip beneath her shawl the scroll she had so patiently and honestly scribbled at—so ashamed of her darling now, so proud of it before—when you saw the gladness go out of her eyes and the tears come there, when she crept away so humbly who had come so—"

My father had described, with startling foresight about our relationship, Twain's relationship with his daughter Susy. He noted how Twain thought she would grow up to be a writer, and how "in everything she did he subjected her to demands for perfection, but he himself was vulnerable to her slightest criticism and was easily angered, pursued by a guilty sense that he had failed her."

In Joe's last months, when I visited the apartment and he could no longer move around easily, when he often fell out of bed at night but refused a railing, when he couldn't hold his gold pencil anymore, he moved from asking me, "What are you reading?" to "What are you writing?"

"More stories," I answered, and changed the subject.

It's only in remembering sitting with him on the balcony, no longer the made-up biographer of a short story but a real one, that I see the bravery in his question, and the suggestion that he was contemplating his limited time left with me. He was braver than I was that day with my opaque answer, but maybe this is the conversation with him I've been waiting for and moving toward as I've written and then imagined handing him these pages. Together, we know that there is nothing more revealing of ourselves than when we talk about what we write, invent, imagine, and hope for.

Fourteen

Going to Space

•

*"After having written about four hundred pages
of manuscript, [Twain] conceded that 'that day's
chapter was a failure . . . and so I must burn up
the day's work and do it all over again. It was
plain that I had worked myself out, pumped myself dry.' Thirty years later he remembered this
crisis as teaching him his great lesson, a basic
tenet of his faith in himself as a writer: 'When
the tank runs dry you've only to leave it alone
and it will fill up again in time.'"*

After his biography of Walt Whitman was published in 1980,
my father set out on the difficult search for his next subject.
There were many starts and as many stops, he said, calling himself "the author of many unwritten books." Twain's
"writing table and manuscript trunk could never hold the
projects he began in a forest fire of enthusiasm and then put
aside, when the flames stopped leaping," he had observed, acknowledging that a writer's material always has to be a bit

on fire if it is going to survive, while also foreshadowing the writer's most dreaded day when his own creativity smolders instead of leaps.

Of his circling around the subject of William James and his ultimate decision not to pursue that biography, he would talk about the "marriage" not working out between them. For a period of time, he thought he might write about Ulysses S. Grant, a man who appears often in the Twain biography. He wrote about the complex intensity of Twain's feelings toward Grant, and that "several levels of relationship can be suggested: the Rebel son and the punishing figure of power and authority . . . the parallel and ironic relationship of anti-hero ('I knew more about retreating than the man who invented retreating') to hero, and humorist to victim." Such psychological investigation might have been applied to his own feelings about Grant as a subject for biography, but he claimed only to have ditched the idea when he discovered that the "great war hero was a much greater judge of horseflesh than of human nature."

Irving Berlin sparked his interest for a while, but his access to the letters between Berlin, a Jew, and his non-Jewish socialite wife—letters expressing the porosity and calcification of class and ethnic lines in the United States in the 1930s—was blocked and killed the deal for him. He had toyed with the idea of biographies of Isabella Stewart Gardner, Frederick Law Olmsted, Winslow Homer, Edgar Allan Poe, Stephen Crane.

And then there was Charlie Chaplin, what looked like his most promising idea. My father spent considerable time and energy in the mid-1980s gaining access to the Chaplin material that was kept in a temperature-controlled vault in Switzerland by Chaplin's widow, Oona. For three weeks, he spent daytime hours in the vault and in the evenings had dinner with her. He must have felt he'd entered the inner sanctum and, in waking every morning to take in the view of Lake Geneva from his hotel room, been energized by the certainty that he'd at last hit upon the subject that would occupy him passionately for years ahead.

Back home in Cambridge, he got to work on Chaplin. The process of necessary entwinement with the man had started: Chaplin ephemera—pictures, movies, books, articles sent by friends and fans, a stuffed doll—filled his study. Months later he emerged with some pages to show my mother. It was a singular, and in retrospect, worrisome event in their long marriage, she told me. While she showed him everything she wrote, he had never shown her his early efforts or his work in progress, always counting on himself to be his own best reader and judge.

There was my father blinking in the sunlight that flooded the kitchen table where they sat with his pages that morning, just as he sat so often with hers. He must have already sensed from her demeanor and solicitousness that what he'd given her wasn't working so that the moment before she spoke had all the terrible burden of the bad news he'd felt lurking outside his study door every day since he'd begun the project. His stomach ached. He had the urge to run out of the house and never come back. He was itchy all over. In this room where he'd spent so much time, had he ever noticed the massive spiderweb in the corner of the ceiling? Had he ever noticed how quiet it was without his daughters, who had moved out years before, or how his wife twirled a finger in her hair as she began to deliver the terrible verdict?

She told him that what he'd written was flat and unconvincing, that it lacked oomph and true engagement; she said she could tell his heart wasn't in it. Today as she recalls how his face fell, there is a rare note of regret in her delivery. She hadn't expected anything from him but brilliance, and what he'd written had taken her by surprise. She hadn't understood until later how his frustrating search leading up to Chaplin had left him fragile and vulnerable and full of doubt, or how worried he was that the real problem might be that he had nothing left to say. To him, it might have seemed as though his pages with all that work and energy of purpose were scattered across the counter, the floor, into the sink with the dirty dishes. An indefatigable writer, he had tried a hundred ways to get at the material, and none of them had worked. He had known this in his core but hoped it wasn't true.

In a book review he'd written for the *Times* a year earlier, his byline had noted that he was "working on a book about Charlie Chaplin." There was always danger in talking about any work in progress; aspirations run the risk of looking like nothing more than hot air and wishful thinking if things don't work out. My father had seen this happen over and over to other writers. But this kind of public declaration is also necessary, in part to gin up the reader's interest, in part to hold the writer to account and finish the damn thing, and in part to give him solid, purposeful ground to go to every morning.

Soon after that morning in the kitchen, my father abandoned the project and later would explain that Chaplin, who had lost his father at an early age, always went back to his childhood in everything he did and as a result his art never grew. "I could have shown that this traumatic boyhood was not only totally formative but supplied the text and subtext for practically every movie Charlie Chaplin ever made," he said in a lecture about the art of biography. "And having made that point, I realized that this was going to be a biography that told the same story over and over again. And that wasn't the kind of book I wanted to write or that you would want to read."

He had run into what he called a deadly biographical paradox with Chaplin, a subject who was "radiantly alive" when performing but insubstantial and uninteresting when he was not. While my father believed that Twain's richest vein of creativity and material was his childhood, Chaplin's tendency toward reiteration instead of reinvention did not sufficiently engage him. And if his greatest connection to his subjects was through their words, and film (or painting, or business, or war, or music) was a different language, he was finally unable to find his own place within the enclosure and form of the man's work. In the end, Joe ended up giving all his material and research to someone who he decided was better suited to write the book.

When I learned that he had given up on the Chaplin project, an image from *The Gold Rush*, which I had watched with him one afternoon, instantly came to mind: Chaplin's character finally getting the cabin door open only to discover that he is hanging over an abyss.

He had been restless the previous summer in Truro, working on the Chaplin book and trying to see what else besides it he could still launch into (near) space. He had discovered that if you lit an M-80 and put an empty coffee can over it, you could blow out the bottom while lifting the rest of it into the air. The convex pieces of metal fell with a swish into the dry beach grass and later came into the house as relics and dishes for olive pits and sea glass. When the electric toothbrush died, he attempted to launch that into space too by planting an explosive under it, and for an instant, it soared, then twisted back to earth.

A novelist who had come for lunch and a swim that day had witnessed this particular space mission, the ignition and the return, and had muttered, "You're going to blow your fucking fingers off."

And then at the end of that summer, my father decided to light a series of the deafening M-80s one night when I was visiting. He would never tell us where he got the things, which led me to imagine him handing over cash to his pusher behind some storied lecture hall at dawn in Harvard Yard. In Cambridge, he would occasionally light one or two at night in the backyard, the sound of the blast echoing off the legacies of the surrounding houses. Windowpanes rattled, the ghosts of the dead stirred, and it was as though my father was trying to shake loose the pressured atmosphere of Francis Avenue—or test again the limits of his acceptance there.

In Truro that night, the explosions echoed round and deep within the locust trees and sand dunes, and more than one neighbor called the local police who drove up the hill with their lights flashing. My father met them at the open front door, shirtless, moths circling the bulb above his head. Had he been setting off firecrackers? they asked. Time and light turned syrupy as I waited to see if he would confess. He looked down at his bare feet and contemplated his choices. He was a kid who'd been caught doing something dangerous and destructive—the risk of fire that summer of drought was very high—but it was still pretty spectacular and satisfying, and the urge to lie was strong. He was the boy again with his homemade slingshot aiming at birds, the boy dropping pennies with his brother from the window, whispering forbidden words. Like Twain, my father "is traveled and worldly, but has an air of surprised innocence and he manages to be a man and a boy at the same time . . . he juggles these vices into seeming merely the habits of a boy playing hooky and fibbing to his mother."

Finally, he stuttered his way through an admission and nodded as the cops warned that if he did it again, they'd arrest him. He came back inside, smirking, and as soon as it could be safely assumed that the police were back out on Route 6, he lit one last M-80. I was sure the police would come back and haul him away. I was furious at his selfish and bad behavior, and that night woke a hundred times thinking the beach grass that surrounded the house was on fire.

———

I had tried to understand where the biographer in my story found himself when he realized he wasn't going to finish his book. "This was news to him until he said it, and it seemed he'd always known this was going to happen. He'd known even as a little boy that it was always just a matter of when he'd arrive at the moment he could no longer force logic out of the dirt. He'd struggled to uncover what his subject had wanted to keep hidden, but he was done now, it was not important, just anxiety cloaked as suspense, as profession."

Years after he'd stopped writing biographies and had turned instead to other forms, he talked and wrote about the challenges of finding the right subject for a biography. The subject must not only engage the biographer's fervent interest but the biographer must also have something new to say, access to some new material or insight, and have an original way to tell the story. Having spent decades plumbing the depths of other men, had Joe's well finally run dry?

"One function of biography as I try to write it," he had said in an interview, "is to find an essential person, the still center of a cluster of identities and presentations of self." I like to think that he had come to see that the final life left to explore with the passion and curiosity and insight he'd brought to understanding the lives of other men was his own. The trick, I want to tell him, is to dig that well deeper and see what rises to fill it up.

Today I am the biographer, not him, and that fiction "The Biographer" feels as much about him as it is about me struggling to uncover my subject and find the essential person, his still center. "Between you and the person you write about there has to be a profoundly intimate, intricate, and endurable link . . . a link of empathy," my father believed, something "as rare as seeing the green flash at sunset or seeing eagles mating in mid-air. It doesn't happen very often."

Fifteen

The View from Here

•

"Was it dream or reality, [Twain] had asked in 1893, that he had been a pilot on the Mississippi and a miner and journalist in Nevada, that he had come East and then sailed to Europe and written a book that made him famous, that he had a wife and children and lived in a villa above Florence? 'This dream goes on and on and on, and sometimes seems so real that I almost believe it is real,' he wrote. 'I wish I knew whether it is a dream or real.'"

One brilliant June afternoon, my father stood on the balcony of the apartment he and my mother had moved to after they sold the house on Francis Avenue. Despite the fact that he used a walker, he'd managed to drag out the telescope on its spindly tripod. By then, he'd been in and out of the hospital for pneumonia and Parkinson's-related problems too many times to remember. The hospital was, in fact, next door and so close that he'd joked about putting up a cable between the two buildings so he could just clip himself in and zip on over when he needed to.

He had written that after Susy's death, Twain "no longer felt that such simple dualities as man and conscience, or Jekyll and Hyde, were adequate solutions to his own enigma, and he turned to psychology, to notions of a 'dream self' and the demonic urgings of the unconscious." Twain's dream stories "deal with the question of guilt and responsibility, with the experience of the destruction of identity and of the sudden recognition of possibility of having never existed at all."

The last time he'd been hospitalized, my father had experienced sundown syndrome, a form of hallucination and dream self. I had been there in his hospital room as he narrated what was going on as though it were happening at that very moment, flying a Blackhawk helicopter over the Charles River (which he could see out the window) and shooting at people with a machine gun while others were shooting at him. Memorial Drive with its line of sycamore trees was scarred and torn up, people desperate for cover. He was so scared it didn't even feel like fear anymore, he said, but he had a job to do. The world was on fire, chaos had taken over, he thought he would soon be killed. Like Twain's dream stories, his had "a tight and urgent coherence: a man makes a spectacular rise to eminence, lives on a plateau of triumph and fulfillment, is betrayed by something within him which he can never discover, and falls."

Twain had written that "from the cradle up I have been like the rest of the race—never quite sane in the night," and on another night, back home from yet another hospital stay, my father had hallucinated that my mother was trying to kill him. He was screaming and agitated, and my mother, terrified, had called the police to help her. "Don't believe a word she says," my father told the cops who stood in his bedroom. "She's a novelist! She makes things up for a living!"

I had been warned by my mother that he was "off his rocker," had screamed at and hit a nurse and fallen out of bed, and I saw from the bruises on his arm, which he waved to imitate the swoop of the helicopter, that he'd been restrained. Twain accepted "the existence of a 'dream self' who comes alive during sleep, is liberated, and does things which the waking self would never dare . . . He appeared at social gatherings dressed only in a nightshirt and told the people, 'I am Mark Twain,' and no one believed him."

My father, once cogent again, was fascinated by his own visions, asking to have them repeated in order to see his liberated self, his unnamable places, his ability to move between reality and delusion. (I didn't tell him about the one incident of hallucination where he looked me straight in the eye and said, "I want to kill you.") What his imagination "released from daytime rationality" had produced, even in delusion, awed him and offered him by way of consolation new ways of seeing himself.

But that day when I joined him on the apartment's balcony, he seemed concerned only with adjusting the telescope that was beyond the ability of his unsteady hands and distorted spatial sense.

"Let me help you," I said. "What are you trying to see?"

"The house," he said.

I trained the telescope in the right direction, but he had to already understand that it was impossible to see Francis Avenue from there. An abundance of trees and the city's density were in the way, and in any case, the curve of the river always pulled the eye toward the more open view.

"It's less than two miles," he said, bent to the eyepiece, "but I should be able to see that far at least."

I recalled how he had written, still as a young man, about Twain's visit to his childhood town of Hannibal: "He arrived on a still Sunday morning. The town seemed deserted. 'Everything was changed,' he noted, 'but when I reached Third or Fourth Street, the tears burst forth and I recognized the mud.'"

A twelve-year-old boy had written to Mark Twain, his hero, to ask, "Would Mr. Twain be willing to change places with him and be a boy again?" He received from Twain an "extraordinarily intimate and revealing letter":

> He would be willing to be a boy again . . . but only under certain conditions . . . eternal summer, with the oleanders in bloom and the sugar cane green, the middle watch in the pilothouse on moonlit nights, friends to talk to and sing with, long trips and short stays in port, a big freight boat that would ignore passenger hails and lay up whenever the fog got thick, and a crew that would never change and never die.

My father would have winced at the obviousness of our moment on the balcony, too easy and with no mystery in the idea that a man, nearing his end, looks back to where he's come from and where he stands now, and finds the distance impossibly short and inconceivably vast at the same time. Much more than two miles and eight decades, everything familiar and unfamiliar at the same time. Still, he recognized the mud. He must have wondered, was the life he'd lived even real?

Six years after the publication of the Twain biography that changed my father's life, we took a family trip to Santa Fe, New Mexico, boarding the Super Chief train that took us overnight from Chicago to Albuquerque. There was a dining car with waiters in uniform, an observation car with windows that rounded toward the roof, and bunks that opened up from the walls of the cabin. The train made frequent stops, and at many of them, my father got off the train to stretch his legs on the platform. I pressed against the window as he wandered out of sight, each time convinced he'd miss the call to reboard.

At dawn, I had woken to see vast plains and the sharp line of the horizon. My father, awake in his bunk, was watching the same view go by. There was not a single break in the landscape, not a tree or a house, just a faint glow at the edge of the earth. You could almost believe the world was flat, that other things you thought were true might not be, and I held in my chest the disquieting possibility of not being myself, of having misplaced my own life.

My father was ostensibly on vacation, but writing a biography (now one of Lincoln Steffens) "was inexorably full-time, even in sleep," and on this trip, even with three children in tow, he was much in his head. I was used to this, but there was something different about his remoteness. One afternoon, we rode on horseback through the Sangre de Cristo Mountains, a name I was excited to learn was inspired by the landscape's various bloody hues. We came across a scattering of hunks of petrified wood. I was told they took millions of years to form, an idea that meant everything and nothing to me. (Later I discovered that my father had pocketed a piece that he brought home to put on his desk. For many years, I worried that the police would show up to arrest him for this.)

While we stopped to admire the scattering of stony wood, my father still on horseback, still an incongruous image, looked out over the scrub and pine. He had been to this same spot years ago, my mother told me then, and I had the sudden sense that if he turned around to look at us, he wouldn't have recognized his own family.

I didn't know then that in his early twenties and baffled by what he'd called "a growing sense of disconnectedness and remoteness" in his graduate studies, my father had taken a leave and gone to Santa Fe for six months. Lonely and unsure of where he belonged or what he would do with his life, he found work at a struggling guest lodge where he cleaned stalls, pumped gas, and tended the garden's chili peppers. His bosses took him for a Scotsman instead of a Jew, at least for a while. His standard college attire of khakis and button-down shirts grew stiff with dust, and his hands blistered from the labor. The rakes and shovels were not pencils and paper. The change of scenery made him thoughtful about the "human order in this New Mexico wilderness as it related to my own feelings of belonging. I lived in a cabin on the edge of a vast national forest bounded by the Sangre de Cristo range," he wrote in *Back Then*. "Possibly no one had ever walked or ridden over much of this land, not even the Indians. Like many other parts of New Mexico, it had remained unexplored for centuries and so 'belonged' to no one, meaning, I supposed, that I had as much a right to be there as anyone."

He did a lot of reading during those solitary months, books that led him to contemplate what it meant to belong— as a man, as a Jew, as himself—and where he might claim his stake, what his own personal frontier, if he could find it, might yield. He saw beyond his cabin door a landscape of an infinite past and a boundless future. But a place void of human footprint and heartbeat—or so he imagined—was also a place fearsomely indifferent to his existence. It might as well have been the moon for all its warmth and familiarity, for all someone might claim him and bring him home.

That day when I looked again at my father on horseback, I knew that he'd been testing the idea of escape all week—on the train platform, and here in the mountains—and thinking about the million other ways in which his life might have gone.

I freeze us both now just before we gaze toward what comes next.

"The drama of literary biography may have less to do with stalking the naked self to its burrow than with the tensions between the familiar, shared life of human beings—making it, making out, making a go of it, making waves, making a name—and a vision so singular it deserves to be regarded with awe," my father wrote in an essay titled "The Naked Self and Other Problems."

Time framed by bloodred stone, my father and I regard the arc of our lives with amazement as we watch our former selves march ahead to deliver us to who we are at this exact moment. I must know and at the same time not know how this all ends in order to write it, in order to see him travel from that moment he looked at the forest beyond his cabin door and contemplated his right to exist to this very instant he exists again in my mind and on this page.

That day with the telescope on the balcony, I wondered if my father was afraid of dying, if he still remembered, like Twain, other views. After all his work to create narratives for his subjects, was my father ready to concede there was no such coherence in life while you were living it? On the first page of Thomas Wolfe's *The Story of a Novel*—a book on whose inside cover my father at the age of eighteen had written "Joseph D. Kaplan 8/31/43"—a single passage is marked by him with the faintest pencil tick, as though he has only an inkling of what's to come and how this might serve as an incitement: "And now I really believe that so far as the artist is concerned, the unlimited extent of human experience is not so important for him as the depth and intensity with which he experiences things."

Recently I watched the only known motion picture of

Mark Twain, made in 1909, a year before he died, using Thomas Edison's Kinetograph camera. (Edison and Twain were friends; my grandfather created the campaign to celebrate the fiftieth anniversary of the electric light and dined with Edison. Maybe over jellied consommé they discussed Twain's mustache.) The movie was filmed at Stormfield, the house in Redding, Connecticut, and the last place Twain lived. He stands at his open front door, and despite his fame, his career as a public figure, and all of his exultant time on stage, he seems uncomfortable. But maybe it's just his unfamiliarity with this particular way of being seen, caught on film. Still, he is aware of the effect of his gaze and looks directly at the camera. He is dressed in white, his linen suit elegantly loose. His hair is white and full and his cigar and shoes provide the only spots of contrast. He's talking, nodding, and ticks his head to his left before he walks down the steps and out of the frame, leaving a view of the screen door and an instant's peek into the dark interior, at the end of which is a glimpse of a window. The entryway's sidelights look remarkably similar to the ones that flanked the front door on Francis Avenue. I'm not struck by any coincidence here—there are a million front doors with sidelights like these—only by my impulse, even now, to step fully into the connections between my father and Twain.

The film moves to Twain rounding the corner of his house on a gravel path, still in the same white suit as he approaches the camera. He's got a funny walk that's almost a waddle, and just before he leaves the frame again, he removes his cigar with a puff of smoke. And then there he is rounding the same corner again, as though the filmmaker and he are giving it another shot; his walk is more confident, he removes his cigar earlier, and just before he passes out of the frame again, one of his daughters, dressed in white, appears for an instant behind the screen door to watch him go. She has either come into the frame by accident or she is a ghost.

Next, Twain and his two daughters, Clara and Jean, appear at an outdoor table. They sit in wicker chairs, the silver tea set in front of them, the daughters with perfect posture, Twain toward the edge of his chair. He holds his tea cup in one hand while the other rests half-fisted on the table. There's a lot of moving of cups to mouths; it looks like a tea-sipping tutorial. Their awkwardness at this moment of filming is clear. Twain says something to make one daughter smile shyly and look down. Behind the three of them and the thick pillars of a large veranda, the trees whip and bend dramatically in the wind. A young man appears for a second to bring one of the daughters her hat, which she puts on and inserts a long pin to hold it in place. There's not much conversation. Twain takes his last sip of tea, pinkie lifted, and then, as if on cue, the three of them rise and walk away.

My father wrote about a day likely not long after the film was made. "At Stormfield in October 1909 [Twain] gathered his scattered and pitifully shrunken family together for the last time. On a clear autumn day . . . Clemens posed with his daughters, his Oxford gown over a white suit, a last flash of brilliant plumage in sunlight." Months later, his daughter Jean would suffer an epileptic seizure and die.

Today I watch the movie again to return to "a last flash of brilliant plumage in sunlight" because it captures Twain in the singular instant, and my father on the balcony, before radiance fades forever.

Sixteen

The River

•

*"In 1909, for Harper's Bazaar, [Twain] wrote
'The Turning-Point of My Life': reviewing his
life and legend once again, he saw everything
he had done and become as predetermined from
the beginning of time, each event only another
link in a chain forged by 'circumstance, working in harness with my temperament'—he
was still pushing away the heavy burden of his
freedom . . . 'My father died this day 63 years
ago,' he wrote to Clara on March 24, 1910, less
than a month before his own death. 'I remember
all about it quite clearly.'"*

Back in his study on Francis Avenue, my father is almost at
the end of the book. I'm almost at the end of mine. He doesn't
know what he'll do next, but today he's not worried.

When Mark Twain died at the age of seventy-four, he had
far surpassed the life expectancy of a man born in 1835. My
father's father died in 1939 at the age of fifty-three. Twenty

years later, my father wrote in his original book proposal that "during the years when the world might have expected him to be happy," Twain was increasingly oppressed by guilt and by a "sense of utter futility and by loneliness . . . And in December 1909, too ill to travel, the old man looked out at the snow storm raging around the house at Redding, while Jean, his last child but one, was taken to burial in Elmira. He lived four months longer."

"The milestones had become gravestones . . . 'The cloud is permanent now.'" It is a heartbreaking admission from Twain, and when my father copies this line onto the page, he is sure that this will not be the story of his own life. He has weathered enough of his own storms to reach this moment when putting another piece of paper in the typewriter has become an act of faith that sustains him.

I'm no longer worried about interrupting him at his desk. He's an acclaimed biographer and he can relax a little. I am decades older than he is and he doesn't yet know how the tide turns at sixty, how the logic of your life can start to ebb. He looks up at me, amused that all those years of trying to keep me out of his study have failed so resoundingly, because here I am, and I didn't even knock first.

Look what I found, I say, and hand him his first book proposal.

I really object to you going through my things.

But you know how that works, I tell him. *Going through other people's things. It's kind of what's required.*

He turns the delicate onionskin pages, the ink so faded it's hard to make out all the words. Writing it was one of the hardest things he'd ever done, he tells me. He seems pleased and surprised by how good and clear it is. *But I had almost no clue what I was doing*, he says, smiling as though he's gotten away with something.

He keeps his eyes on the pages as I tell him how I think one of the reasons he chose to write about Twain was because the man had lived a long life, and Joe had no models for that. I suggest that he would not have spent all those years with Twain if the man hadn't shown him how to survive.

You should have been a shrink, or a pathologist, he says, perhaps remembering what Twain had written about Susy in the foreword of her biography of him: "Like other children, she was blithe and happy, fond of play; unlike the average of children, she was at times much given to retiring within herself and trying to search out the hidden meanings of the deep things that make the puzzle and the pathos of human existence and in all the ages have baffled the inquirer and moved him."

Let me read to you from your own book for a minute. I have my copy with me, fattened by the hundreds of Post-its on the pages.

No, thank you. Let's play Ping-Pong. Or take a walk?

He stands, but I tell him to sit.

[Livy and Clara] were still on the high seas on August 18 when, as Clemens stood in the dining room at Guildford thinking about nothing in particular, he was handed a cable that told him Susy, twenty-four years old, had died of meningitis. "It is one of the mysteries of our nature," he reflected when nearly ten years had gone by, "that a man, all unprepared can receive a thunder-stroke like that and live."

To write this, I tell him, he must have pictured Twain contemplating the view and the summer light, doing more sensing than thinking. He must have seen Twain with one hand in a pocket of a linen jacket, the other holding a cigar. He knows how Twain notices the sound an empty house holds because he experiences it himself in the rare and valuable instances he's alone in this big house. It is in this state that the thunder-strike finds its power to kill.

And yet it doesn't, Joe says. *People survive all sorts of things.*

"The summer before, he had made notes for a story about life in the interior of an iceberg which drifts in a vast circle year after year for 130 years, by which time generations of people inside are dead and frozen; he would return to this theme after Susy died," I read to him. "In January 1885, as if anticipating just such a loss, he translated into English the last part of a German prose version of 'The Pied Piper.' He called this episode 'The Great Loneliness'; the mothers wake out of sleep, push open the doors of their children's rooms, see that the beds are still empty and always will be, call out in a last hope, and then turn away—'Ah, dear God, if it could have been but a dream.'"

I tell him how I cried reading his description of the death of Twain's infant son Langdon, a "fat, alabaster-white baby" who had been seriously ill a number of times before his father took him out one morning for a long drive in an open carriage.

I read a passage to him: "[Twain] fell into 'a reverie,' he said many years later, and let the fur blankets slip off Langdon." The child, who was "almost frozen died not of pneumonia but of diphtheria . . . [which] fails to jibe with [Twain's] statement that he was responsible for the boy's death . . . looking back on that carriage ride with Langdon, [Twain] wrote in 1906: 'I have always felt shame for that treacherous morning's work and have not allowed myself to think of it when I could help it.'"

Well, that was a very sad thing, my father says. We are both thinking of our own children in this moment. *He blamed himself for a lot.*

I point out how grief marches through his book, animated. It is the starting gun at the race, the runner in first place, the runner coming up fast in second, and the finish line all at once: "At York Harbor, Maine, in the summer of 1902, [Twain] watched helpless as Livy lapsed into her last illness," he had written. And then later, when it was clear that she had given up, she talked about the lavender satin dress she wanted to be buried in. "After a brief remission, when she suddenly looked bright and young again, [Twain] saw in her gaze 'that pathetic something . . . which betrays the secret of a waning hope.'"

I don't tell my father how when I read those pages about Livy's decline, I read them as though they were the account of his own mother's death. My grandmother's face in my father's eye had long ago faded, but here was the longing reignited in writing about another man's experience.

What's your point? my father asks, warily.

What were you doing when your mother died? I ask.

He doesn't hesitate. *I was five. No, six. I don't know how old I was,* he says. *The only thing I remember is that right after she died, I pushed open her eyelids. I was trying to see if she was just asleep.*

As they carried her out on a stretcher to the hospital before she died, his mother had cried, "I'm too young to die," he tells me.

"For years, side by side with a photograph of my best dog ever, I've kept on my office mantelpiece Mathew Brady's portrait of the eleven-year-old Henry James and his father," my father had written in 2004. "The boy wears a tight-fitting jacket with a line of brass buttons running up the front. His right hand rests on his father's left shoulder in a delicate gesture of intimacy and trust. His eyes are fixed in the spectral stare . . . But I like to think that we can see even then the eyes of the great novelist who dedicated himself to being (in his words) 'one of the people on whom nothing is lost.'"

I point to the picture on his desk of him and his father, Tobias, walking in 1938, the year before his father died. My father looks happy in the photograph, knobby-kneed and secure that his father is looking ahead on the country road for oncoming cars so that he can gaze to the side and see what's out there in the fields as they walk. Nothing is lost on him. Both of them have walking sticks. Howard must have taken the picture, and all three of them must have imagined a time in the future when they'd look at it and try to remember the circumstances of the day, when they might, as Twain described in *The Innocents Abroad*, "have forgotten all the sorrows and

privations of that canonized epoch and remember only its or-
chard robberies, its wooden sword pageants and its fishing
holydays,"

This is what you will write about your father years from now, I
tell him. He is pensive, twirling his gold pencil. "My brother
and I were the absolute center, the true north, of his life and
affections. Even in early middle age and excellent health
making provisions for them after his death was his driving
concern."

Those are my private notes, he says.

I found them in the red binder, the one you left for me to find,
I remind him.

All this probing, pushing, my wild assumptions about
him—he's getting heated. Cast in the role of the pursued subject, he perhaps remembers he'd written that "one can't blame
these fugitives—they knew that even the best-disposed biographies have to have an adversary or inquisitorial aspect if
they are to arrive at any kind of truth."

*Your father was possibly already sick when the picture was
taken*, I say. *Do you think he knew?*

No. Probably. He tilts his head left and right, as though trying to find some balance for what he knows is the truth. *In
some way. He must have. Yes.*

Tobias's walking stick, the one still in my father's study,
would hardly protect the boys from anything.

And did you *know? Did you also see "that pathetic something . . . which betrays the secret of a waning hope"? Did you
know it because you'd seen it before?*

Jesus Christ. Stop. This is not how biography works. He gives me a look; he's irritated by my lack of discipline. *That was Twain's life, not mine. You're making a mistake going down this path.* He shakes his head and stands. *I really object to this.* He wipes the dust off the leaves of a rubber plant with the hem of his shirt. He looks into the weedy overgrowth of the side yard.

I read to him about Twain sitting at the bedside of his dying father-in-law.

> Characteristically, what [Twain] remembered years later with agonizing clarity was the guilt of "my noddings, my fleeting unconsciousness, when the fan would come to a standstill in my hand and I would wake up with a start and a hideous shock."

Is there always guilt in a bedside vigil? I ask.

It's hard to ever feel you've done or said enough.

You wrote that on his deathbed at Mount Sinai Hospital, your father recited Psalm 22: "Why hast thou forsaken me?"

Joe looks at me blankly.

So, you were there, I say.

I guess I was.

I won't remind him of what he'd written in his notes: "I'm fascinated by the realization that I am now much older than my parents: how does this seniority mesh with the realization one is always going to be a child to and with one's parents?"

I won't tell him that when he is in the hospital for the last time, I will bring with me for fun a copy of *Advanced College Entrance Reviews in English Aptitude* from 1970, which I'd kept for no reason I can understand except that I might have foreseen this exact moment. Even in his mildly sedated state, he is excited to be tested on some analogies:

1. GENESIS; DEMISE (1) inception: termination (2) omega: alpha (3) dawn: prime (4) abyss: acme.

2: EJACULATE; WHISPER (1) prove: admonish (2) vociferate: utter (3) scream: moan (4) murmur: mutter.

There is no answer key in the book and we are both hopeless with analogies. He aces the vocabulary and I can't stump him on anything: termagant—boisterous, domineering woman; poltroon—coward.

I won't tell him that the last thing he'll say to me on his deathbed is "See you tomorrow."

What are you after here? Can we cut to the chase, please? he says. He cautions me against writing a pathography, a life account that makes you wonder how the subject even managed to get out of bed in the morning, much less write a book or function in the world. *Sad things happen. You move on. Enough with the melodrama.*

Why have I brought him to this moment? I read another passage he wrote about Twain after Jean died: "On Christmas Day, too ill to travel, Clemens stood at the window and watched the hearse moving downhill through a heavy snowstorm. 'I have never greatly envied any one but the dead,' he said. 'I always envy the dead.'"

Joe stands to look out the window onto Francis Avenue. He can't imagine the changes that will happen here, the ones he won't live to see, like the transformation of this study into a media room with a giant TV hung over the fireplace, his books replaced by arty brass orbs and pale, unkillable succulents. When he and my mother leave the house, it will be his books he mourns the most openly; there is not enough room for them in the new apartment. The rare book dealer will break the news to him that all his collections and his curated library are of almost no value. No one wants books anymore, unless they're bought in bulk and by the pound for decoration.

Joe won't see how the renovated houses on the street will start to have the same rictus-like tightness of the just face-lifted who secretly miss their old, recognizable selves when they look in the mirror. Front doors will finally shut tight, the pipes will be sleek and soundless, sprinkler systems will hiss on at 4:00 a.m. His own memorial service will be held down the street in a building owned by Harvard, and his many, many friends, colleagues, admirers, and people who sat in his study and kitchen table and asked him how to get the job of writing done, will get up and tell stories about him, his humor, his warmth, his generosity, his mind, and his writing.

He won't live to see that not a single one of these stories will include anything about his children or about him as a father.

I read to him: "In Hannibal, Mark Twain could believe he was a boy again, a boy who had never left the town in 1853 to set out on his travels but instead had a dream twenty-nine years long about growing up. He woke up each morning a boy, but at night, after visiting with old friends who were rich or fat or grizzled and had children long since grown up and gone away, he went to bed feeling a hundred years old. 'That world which I knew in its blossoming youth is old and bowed and melancholy now,' he wrote to Livy. 'It will be dust and ashes when I come again. I have been clasping hands with the moribund—and usually they say, 'It is for the last time.'"

I need to walk the dog, Joe says, though the animal is fast asleep and slow to stir.

He puts a leash on her and we leave the house, cutting through Harvard Yard and making our way to the Charles River. When I was a kid, the river was highly toxic from polluted storm water and urban runoff. Standing at one end of Harvard Square, you could easily get a fetid whiff of it and, on its banks, find dead fish in the reeds. Once, getting too close to examine the single eye of a floater, I'd almost fallen in, but my father had caught me. I'd been told that if you were unlucky or drunk enough to tumble into the river, you might die. Even a few drops of it in your mouth would send you to the hospital, your future touch and go.

The river is cleaner these days and for a while we watch the rowers. My father asks me if I'm familiar with the paintings of Thomas Eakins. He tells me he'd thought about writing a biography of the guy at one point, but he didn't think he could find a way to penetrate the magnificence of the art, and as he stands there watching the boats slice through the water, he seems to be still working at that translation problem. It has always been what has fueled him.

"Two currents flowed though Mark Twain's life," he wrote. "One flowed outward and away from the river town of Hannibal, Missouri, toward the nation and the world; the other flowed back home again." The moment the currents collided is the moment he decided to make a writer's life out of a storm. Biography, my father had said, is an antidote to loneliness and a restorative of solitude. Maybe the orphan, like the writer, never gives up his need for solitude; maybe solitude never gives up its hold on him. Even as his family waits for him on the other side of the door.

"We tend to assume," he wrote, ". . . that we are looking for a 'core' in biography, a naked self, an unmoving mover . . . this core may be only the sum of many 'presentations of self,' interactions, gestures, codes, and signifiers. The real me of creative people may be found only in the making of the work and in the work itself."

The real me is in writing about him and the making of this work, where I find my own acceptance. My father was the man who listened to Verdi and Jacques Brel and was moved to tears as he stood alone in the kitchen watering his rangy plants at the back of the room, who confessed to a friend that he delighted in driving his daughters to school so he could listen to their unguarded talk. He was the sensitive photographer who captured his children's essence so completely that even today the pictures startle me with evidence of his wells of affection and observation, even as he remained resolutely opaque; me at four on the other side of a chain-link fence, looking through at him.

My father was the man who told two stories about himself but didn't see the pattern of invisibility, attack, visibility, and retreat. One was about coming out of a store in Boston to find that he'd been boxed in by a car parked too close behind him. After spending many minutes maneuvering his car out, he found a full trash can and dumped its contents on the offending driver's windshield before speeding away. The other was about a New York City bus driver who had called my newly parentless father a dirty kike. When my father got off the bus at his stop, he gave the driver the finger and ran faster than he'd ever run before while the driver chased but never caught him.

He was the man sensitive to slight and rejection—you could see it in his eyes, always cautious, always looking away first—who charmed with his gentleness, attentiveness, humor and flirtation. He was the man who in any department store would spritz himself with a dozen different perfumes for fun. He was so inept at fixing anything that he could not change a light bulb or insert a battery, but a single hour with him, his prose, his ear and eye and his gold pencil would make you a better and smarter and more thoughtful writer for the rest of your life.

I remind him of this: One night when I was thirteen, when you and my mother were out at some party and Susanna and Polly were upstairs in their rooms—we were always three girls in three separate universes—I stood at your closed study door. The dog wandered up behind me, dumbly waiting to be let in, but I left her out in the hall; I didn't want a witness. Inside, I took a seat in your chair, turned on the fancy IBM Selectric, and touched the side of the machine to feel its purr. It made a satisfying clunk when I turned it on and off, on and off. I opened your desk drawer, swirled a finger through the paperclips, rolled the pens, stretched the rubber bands, looked at a yellowed photograph of a woman I didn't recognize in a cinch-waisted plaid coat and closed the drawer. You had an ancient rubber glue dispenser with a brush built into the lid from your very first job in publishing, its brown glass jar pimpled irresistibly with sticky drippings to pick off and roll into tiny balls. The smell was sweet, intoxicating, and vaguely dangerous and I inhaled deeply.

I swiveled around and around in the chair, and when my hand swept through a stack of index cards, I watched them float indifferently through the air. Panicked, I was sure speed was the solution to the damage I'd just caused, and that if I dropped to my knees and gathered the cards up quickly enough, then there would be no harm done. I moved fast to put them in order, but they were not numbered or coded. I couldn't make out your scratchy handwriting, words, sentences, dates that might suggest some logic. I was sure I had destroyed if not the whole of the new book you were working on, then at least something critically important. There would be no way to repair what I'd broken, no way to escape my rotten, destructive nature. There was suddenly every reason why the room was off-limits to me.

Later in the dark of my bedroom where I shivered with distress, I heard you come home around midnight. I will lie and say it wasn't me, I decided. No, I will confess and say I'd just come in looking for some paper, and that it was an accident. No, it would be better to convince myself that I'd never even been in your study, that this simply had never happened. The next morning at breakfast, you folded the newspaper with the precision of origami, read details from an obituary you liked, drank your coffee, let the dog in and out, loaded the dishwasher, tossed a ball with us outside before the carpool to school arrived. You had not yet been in your study that morning, but when you emerged from it late after a day of writing, I saw that you knew exactly what I had done, that it could only have been me, a child with a reputation for sneakiness, a child who snooped into everything and eavesdropped from the back stairway, who broke into hidden closets, and held her secrets close. When you looked at me, you held your gaze for an extra second, something so rare I knew I had to be right.

Yes, I knew it was you, he says, smiling. *Of course I knew it was you. Who else could it be?*

I thought that I'd destroyed your book, I say.

You didn't. Nothing was lost. Maybe you even made it better, tossed things up a bit.

I just wanted to understand how it's done, why it works. He shrugs as if to suggest that's the mystery we're all after and the one we won't solve.

Shame is a persistent ember, I tell him, and it found its way into "The Biographer." But in the story, the shame also belongs to the father as he remembers the moment he discovers his burglar daughter "on all fours in his study, surrounded by paper clips she couldn't manage to pick up. She was made inept with the guilt of trespassing. Her curls were tinged with gold. He'd swung his foot to her bottom not with a kick, nothing hard or violent, but with enough intent that her hands and arms splayed, she toppled forward, and her chest and chin hit the floor. He smelled the old walls baking in the heat. After a second, she raised herself and crawled out of the room, never looking back at him. They never spoke about it."

I never did that, he says, his eyes tearing. *I would never, ever do that.*

When you held my criminal gaze that evening, I tell him, it was suddenly clear to me that you hadn't told my mother, and I felt then a kind of dented relief that this would stay between the two of us. For you to keep this from her, when you two always presented an impenetrable unified front, spoke to some new understanding you had about me. And when I read, years later as I began this book and opened your biography of Mark Twain for the first time, that you had written, "At the age of thirteen, Susy Clemens, a fascinated observer of her father's moods and fluctuations, began to write his 'biography,'" I felt the breath of your prescience. Something in your sense of me shifted that day because you understood what it meant to search for someone. That you always knew I would write this story of you, that I would pick up and reorder those index cards.

I ask him if I've discovered enough to write about him.

Who knows? You can find a lot and still not know all that much, he laughs. *That's the reality of it. Anyway, it's not just what you found or didn't find, it's how you put the pieces of a life together, how* you *made it make sense, how* you *wrote the story, how* you *know me. It was always about you and your search, even if in the end, we are always still unknown to ourselves.*

Reading Susy's biography of him, years after she was gone, Twain had written that "after all these many years, it is still a king's message to me and brings me to the same dear surprise it brought me then—with the pathos added of the thought that the eager and heavy hand that sketched it and scrawled it will not touch mine again."

If he were a different person, my father might say he understands it was the greatest act of love for me to write about him, that it was my way of finding him. But he doesn't talk like that and says instead, *Would you like me to read what you've written?*

His hands are open. I feel that same seizing of fear, of exposure of myself, but he is not vapor or smoke anymore.

He holds these pages now, proof that he was always my material waiting to be found and delivered and my way to this moment of conclusion for the two of us. In his eighties, he had scribbled on the back of an envelope notes for a summer class on biography he was going to teach to adults, evidence of the persistence of questions that occupied him about how we write and understand the stories of life: "Does life itself have a form? Does life have a theme, a plot, a structure? Do lives have turning points? Or are these extracted from life or imposed upon it?"

He points to a boat that has turned sideways in the river, the rower trying to right herself again. It's hard to know, we agree, how she found herself in this peculiar position when the current had been pointing her in the right direction.

When you look closely, he says, all lives are spectacular, all lives are mysteries too sacred to be solved. They are mysteries to be regarded with awe.

Acknowledgments

To my friends who listened with endless patience, asked tough and necessary questions, and offered me ways ahead in this book: David Elliott, Jo-Anne Hart, Michael Lowenthal, Elizabeth Keithline, Nancy Reisman.

To my mother and my sisters for their stories: Anne Bernays, Polly Kaplan, Susanna Kaplan, and to the literary estate of Justin Kaplan.

To my editors, Elizabeth Pankova and Kendall Storey, whose deeply intelligent and sensitive work on this book helped me discover what I was trying to say—and then helped me say it in better and braver ways. I am forever grateful. To be in the hands of such skilled and attentive editors is a writer's dream.

To my agent, Jennifer Carlson, profound thanks for her generous presence, her abundant smarts, support, and guidance for many years. A writer should never run out of words, but there are not enough of them to express my gratitude.

To the team at Catapult who handled my book with great care and attention: Lena Moses-Schmitt, Lily Philpot, Rachel Fershleiser, Wah-Ming Chang, Nicole Caputo, and Victoria Maxfield for her beautiful cover.

For their counsel, conversation, insight, and encouragement: Megan Marshall, Larry Tye, Annie Dillard. Joseph Finder, Kyoko Mori, Jane Brox, Sinan Unel, Pamela Petro, Peter Kramer, Rachel Schwartz, Deborah Corey, Doris Held, Julia Held, Taylor Roberts, Jerome Loving, the late Stephen Lieber, Taylor Polites, Diana Champa, Anna Rosenblum, Janet Sylvester, David Weitz, Laura Wald, *The Ocean State Review*.

For their gift of support, time, and space, my thanks to: The National Endowment for the Arts, Monson Arts, the Fellowship at Quarry Farm and the Center for Mark Twain Studies, Vermont Studio Center.

To Tobias and Alexander, the love and the fuel for everything I write, and to Sofia, Roy, and my heart, Alia. You can enter my study anytime. To Michael, my first, my truest, my best reader, my love and my companion on the road ahead.

HESTER KAPLAN is the author of novels and story collections, including *The Edge of Marriage*, winner of the Flannery O'Connor Award for Short Fiction. Her fiction and nonfiction have appeared in literary journals and anthologies, including *The Best American Short Stories*. She is the recipient of two National Endowment for the Arts awards and was named a Center for Mark Twain Studies Quarry Farm Fellow for *Twice Born*.